*Especially for*

..............................................................................................

*From*

..............................................................................................

*Date*

..............................................................................................

# *My Prayer*
# JOURNAL

Mornings with God

BARBOUR BOOKS
An Imprint of Barbour Publishing, Inc.

Published by Barbour Books, an imprint of Barbour Publishing, Inc., P.O. Box 719, Uhrichsville, Ohio 44683, www.barbourbooks.com

*Our mission is to publish and distribute inspirational products offering exceptional value and biblical encouragement to the masses.*

 Member of the
Evangelical Christian
Publishers Association

Printed in China.

## *Introduction*

As women seeking to live out our faith in a busy world, we simply must begin each day in the presence of God. He longs to make Himself known to us. *My Prayer Journal: Mornings with God* is a collection of prayers, scriptures, and brief devotions designed to help you start each morning with the Lord. As you read the prayer selections, write your own prayers in the journaling sections. Meditate on the scriptures. God loves you, and He desires daily fellowship with you. You are a daughter of the King of kings. Begin each morning with your Father.

*And in the morning, rising up a great while*
*before day, he went out, and departed into a*
*solitary place, and there prayed.*
MARK 1:35

# Joy Comes in the Morning

*Good morning, God! How many nights will I cry myself to sleep before I remember that Your Word promises joy when I wake? In the darkness of the night, my troubles seem insurmountable. But they're not. Everything seems fresh in the morning. I realize once again that together, we can do this. Thank You, Father, for a new day! May I discover true joy in it. Amen.*

When worry overwhelms you in the darkness, trust what God has shown you to be true in the light. Each day His mercies are new!

........................................................................................

........................................................................................

........................................................................................

........................................................................................

........................................................................................

........................................................................................

........................................................................................

........................................................................................

........................................................................................

........................................................................................

........................................................................................

........................................................................................

*Weeping may endure for a night,*
*but joy cometh in the morning.*
PSALM 30:5

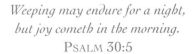

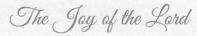

# The Joy of the Lord

*Lord, some mornings I wake up ready to go! I feel rested and energetic.*
*Other mornings, I wonder how I will make it through the day.*
*Remind me that as Your child, I have a power source that is always*
*available to me. I may not always feel joyful, but the joy of the*
*Lord is my strength. As I spend time in Your Word, renew my*
*strength, I pray. In Jesus' name, amen.*

Those who read and meditate upon the Word of the Lord
know His heart in a unique way. True joy comes through a
relationship with the Father.

........................................................................................................

........................................................................................................

........................................................................................................

........................................................................................................

........................................................................................................

........................................................................................................

........................................................................................................

........................................................................................................

........................................................................................................

........................................................................................................

........................................................................................................

........................................................................................................

........................................................................................................

*For the joy of the LORD is your strength.*
NEHEMIAH 8:10

# True Joy

*Thank You, Father, for Your Word, which teaches me how to experience true joy. This world sends me a lot of messages through the media and through those who do not know You. I have tried some of the things that are supposed to bring joy, but they always leave me empty in the end. Thank You for the truth. Help me to abide in You, that I might be overflowing with joy. Amen.*

Did you realize that Jesus Christ wants you to be *full* of joy? Even *overflowing* with joy? Read John 15, which teaches how to be joy-filled.

*These things have I spoken unto you, that my joy might remain in you, and that your joy might be full.*
JOHN 15:11

# Joyful in Hope

*God, the longer I live, the more I realize that joy and hope go hand in hand. I have joy because my hope is in You. Thank You, Lord, that as Your daughter, I do not go out to face the day in hopelessness. No matter what happens, I can find joy because my hope is not in this world or in my circumstances. My hope is in the Lord. Amen.*

Those who trust in the name of the Lord are set apart. There is joy in the countenance of a believer that does not shine forth from the face of the hopeless.

...................................................................................................................

...................................................................................................................

...................................................................................................................

...................................................................................................................

...................................................................................................................

...................................................................................................................

...................................................................................................................

...................................................................................................................

...................................................................................................................

...................................................................................................................

...................................................................................................................

...................................................................................................................

...................................................................................................................

*Happy is he that hath the God of Jacob for*
*his help, whose hope is in the LORD his God.*
PSALM 146:5

# Joy in the Name of the Lord

*Father, this morning I meet You here for just a few moments before the busyness of the day takes over. I trust You. It is not always easy to trust, but You have proven trustworthy in my life. I find joy in the knowledge that You are my defender. You go before me this day into battle. I choose joy today because I love the name of the Lord Almighty. Amen.*

What joy there is in this: If you are a daughter of the Sovereign God, you never have to wonder if He will be there for you. He is trustworthy.

*But let all those that put their trust in thee rejoice:*
*let them ever shout for joy, because thou defendest them:*
*let them also that love thy name be joyful in thee.*
PSALM 5:11

# Joyful Regardless of Circumstances

*Lord, there are days when I can't help but rejoice in what You are doing. But many times the daily grind is just rather humdrum. There is nothing to rejoice about, much less give thanks for! Or is there? Help me, Father, to be joyful and thankful every day. Each day is a gift from You. Remind me of this truth today, and give me a joyful, thankful heart, I ask. Amen.*

Do you know someone who is always wearing a smile? That individual has made a choice to be joyful regardless of circumstances. *Choose* to have a joyful, thankful attitude.

........................................................................................

........................................................................................

........................................................................................

........................................................................................

........................................................................................

........................................................................................

........................................................................................

........................................................................................

........................................................................................

........................................................................................

........................................................................................

........................................................................................

........................................................................................

........................................................................................

........................................................................................

*Rejoice evermore. Pray without ceasing. In every thing give thanks: for this is the will of God in Christ Jesus concerning you.*
1 THESSALONIANS 5:16–18

# Joyful in Song

*Heavenly Father, this morning I come to You with a song on my lips and joy in my heart. I thank You for all that You are doing in my life. You are at work when I sense Your presence and even when I don't. I praise You for being God. I rejoice because I am Your daughter. Amen.*

The Bible speaks of rejoicing with song, praising God through music, and even dancing before the Lord. How will you praise your heavenly Father today through music?

.......................................................................................................................
.......................................................................................................................
.......................................................................................................................
.......................................................................................................................
.......................................................................................................................
.......................................................................................................................
.......................................................................................................................
.......................................................................................................................
.......................................................................................................................
.......................................................................................................................
.......................................................................................................................
.......................................................................................................................
.......................................................................................................................
.......................................................................................................................

*The LORD is my strength and my shield; my heart trusted in him, and I am helped: therefore my heart greatly rejoiceth; and with my song will I praise him.*
PSALM 28:7

# No More Sorrow

*Jesus, Your disciples were dismayed. You told them You were going away but that You would see them again. Those men had walked and talked with You. You were their leader, their friend. How lost they must have felt at Your crucifixion! But three days later. . . Wow! Lord, You turn mourning into rejoicing. Help me to trust in this. Thank You, Jesus. Amen.*

Today your heart may be heavy with loss or longing. One day there will be no more sorrow, only joy! Claim this promise from God's Word.

................................................................................................................

................................................................................................................

................................................................................................................

................................................................................................................

................................................................................................................

................................................................................................................

................................................................................................................

................................................................................................................

................................................................................................................

................................................................................................................

................................................................................................................

................................................................................................................

*And ye now therefore have sorrow: but I
will see you again, and your heart shall rejoice,
and your joy no man taketh from you.*
JOHN 16:22

# Joy in God's Word

*Thank You, God, that in Your holy scriptures I find the ways of life. I find wise counsel on the pages of my Bible. You reveal the truth to me, Lord, and there is no greater blessing than to know the truth. You tell me in Your Word that the truth sets me free. I am free to live a life that brings You glory and honor. May others see the joy I have found in You! Amen.*

God may not write the answers to your questions in the sky, but they are written on the pages of His timeless, truth-filled Word.

...........................................................................................................
...........................................................................................................
...........................................................................................................
...........................................................................................................
...........................................................................................................
...........................................................................................................
...........................................................................................................
...........................................................................................................
...........................................................................................................
...........................................................................................................
...........................................................................................................
...........................................................................................................
...........................................................................................................

*Thou hast made known to me the ways of life;*
*thou shalt make me full of joy with thy countenance.*
ACTS 2:28

# Glorifying God in My Work

*God, today as I work both in my home and outside of it, may my attitude glorify You. I am not of this world, but I am in it, and often it has too much influence on me. May I think twice before I grumble, Father, about the tasks set before me this day. I will choose to work as unto my Father, and may my countenance reflect Your love to those around me. Amen.*

God ordained that mankind should work and then rest. He modeled this for us in His creation of the world. Work. . .because God calls us to do so.

................................................................................

................................................................................

................................................................................

................................................................................

................................................................................

................................................................................

................................................................................

................................................................................

................................................................................

................................................................................

................................................................................

................................................................................

*And whatsoever ye do, do it heartily, as to the Lord, and not unto men; knowing that of the Lord ye shall receive the reward of the inheritance; for ye serve the Lord Christ.*
COLOSSIANS 3:23–24

## Serve One Another

*God, I have not been put on this earth to serve myself. It is not all about me. Sometimes I forget that! Service is what this life is all about, isn't it? Father, give me opportunities to show love to others today. Make every moment a "God moment." Help me to be aware of the many needs around me. Create in me a heart that loves others and puts them ahead of myself. Amen.*

Consider your motive for service. Are you serving others because you want to be noticed for your kindness? Or are you serving others in love and true compassion?

........................................................................................................

........................................................................................................

........................................................................................................

........................................................................................................

........................................................................................................

........................................................................................................

........................................................................................................

........................................................................................................

........................................................................................................

........................................................................................................

........................................................................................................

........................................................................................................

*For, brethren, ye have been called unto liberty; only use not liberty for an occasion to the flesh, but by love serve one another. For all the law is fulfilled in one word, even in this; Thou shalt love thy neighbour as thyself.*
GALATIANS 5:13–14

# Opportunities to Serve

*Father, with this new day, give me new eyes. Show me the hungry,*
*the lonely, the tired. Show me those who need encouragement,*
*those who need a friend, those who need to see Jesus in me. I don't*
*want to miss the chances that You give me to be a blessing to others.*
*I know that when I serve others, the heart of my Creator is blessed.*
*Make me aware of others' needs, I ask. Amen.*

Today offer a smile or a hug. Give away your time, talents, or
resources. It will come back to you tenfold in the blessing you
receive for serving others.

...................................................................................................................

...................................................................................................................

...................................................................................................................

...................................................................................................................

...................................................................................................................

...................................................................................................................

...................................................................................................................

...................................................................................................................

...................................................................................................................

...................................................................................................................

...................................................................................................................

...................................................................................................................

*And the King shall answer and say unto them,*
*Verily I say unto you, Inasmuch as ye have done it unto*
*one of the least of these my brethren, ye have done it unto me.*
MATTHEW 25:40

# Putting God First

*Father, a glance at my bank statement causes me to shudder. Where does my money go? Am I too concerned with what the world says I must possess to be cool, to fit in, to appear successful? Your Word says that I cannot serve both material wealth and You. I choose You, Lord. Be the master of my life and of my checkbook. I need Your help with this. Amen.*

God knows this world sends you a lot of messages. He understands temptation. Call on Him to help you make wise financial decisions. Put Him first, and He will provide all that you need.

.......................................................................................
.......................................................................................
.......................................................................................
.......................................................................................
.......................................................................................
.......................................................................................
.......................................................................................
.......................................................................................
.......................................................................................
.......................................................................................
.......................................................................................
.......................................................................................
.......................................................................................

*No man can serve two masters: for either he will hate the one, and love the other; or else he will hold to the one, and despise the other. Ye cannot serve God and mammon.*
MATTHEW 6:24

# Showing Mercy

*Jesus, like the Good Samaritan in Your parable, may I, too,
show mercy. Some may never enter the doors of a church, but what a
difference an act of grace could make! Put before me opportunities to
show unmerited favor. That is, after all, what You have shown to me.
You died for my sins. I could never have earned salvation. It is a
free gift, an act of grace. Make me merciful. Amen.*

Two other men saw the man who had fallen among thieves.
Will you pass by, as they did, when you see someone in need?
Or will you show mercy like the Good Samaritan?

........................................................................................................

........................................................................................................

........................................................................................................

........................................................................................................

........................................................................................................

........................................................................................................

........................................................................................................

........................................................................................................

........................................................................................................

........................................................................................................

........................................................................................................

........................................................................................................

*Which now of these three, thinkest thou, was neighbour unto him
that fell among the thieves? And he said, He that shewed mercy on him.
Then said Jesus unto him, Go, and do thou likewise.*
LUKE 10:36–37

# What Would Jesus Do?

*Heavenly Father, sometimes I am a Sunday Christian. How I want to worship You with the rest of my week! Please help me to be mindful of You throughout the week. May Your will and Your ways permeate my thoughts and decisions. Whether I am taking care of things at home or working with others in the workplace, may I glorify You in all that I say and do. Amen.*

As you go about your daily activities, remember the Lord. Do everything with Him in mind. WWJD: *What would Jesus do?*

........................................................................

........................................................................

........................................................................

........................................................................

........................................................................

........................................................................

........................................................................

........................................................................

........................................................................

........................................................................

........................................................................

........................................................................

........................................................................

........................................................................

*Whether therefore ye eat, or drink,*
*or whatsoever ye do, do all to the glory of God.*
1 CORINTHIANS 10:31

# Use Me, Lord

*Savior, You laid down Your life for me. You died a horrible death upon a cross. It was death by crucifixion, which was reserved for the worst of criminals. And You had done nothing wrong. You came into the world to save us! You gave Your very life for us. Jesus, take my life. Use me for Your kingdom's work. Only in losing my life for You will I save it. Amen.*

Jesus was a servant king. The world looked for grandeur but found Him riding on the back of a donkey and ministering to society's lowlifes. Serve as Jesus modeled.

...................................................................................................................

...................................................................................................................

...................................................................................................................

...................................................................................................................

...................................................................................................................

...................................................................................................................

...................................................................................................................

...................................................................................................................

...................................................................................................................

...................................................................................................................

...................................................................................................................

...................................................................................................................

...................................................................................................................

...................................................................................................................

*For whosoever will save his life shall lose it; but whosoever shall lose his life for my sake and the gospel's, the same shall save it.*
MARK 8:35

# A Giving Heart

*Father, may I be honest? Sometimes I don't feel like serving. They keep asking if I will help with this or that at church. And there is always a collection being taken up. Can't I just focus on me? I have my own needs! But oh, the peace I feel when I lay my head on my pillow at night knowing I have loved with action, with sacrifice. Make me a giver, I ask. Amen.*

The very richest people in the world are those who give it all away. There is a joy in generosity that the stingy forfeit with every coin saved.

.........................................................................................................................................
.........................................................................................................................................
.........................................................................................................................................
.........................................................................................................................................
.........................................................................................................................................
.........................................................................................................................................
.........................................................................................................................................
.........................................................................................................................................
.........................................................................................................................................
.........................................................................................................................................
.........................................................................................................................................
.........................................................................................................................................
.........................................................................................................................................

*Remember the words of the Lord Jesus, how he said,
It is more blessed to give than to receive.*
ACTS 20:35

# Glorifying God

*Father, I tend to seek the glory for myself. It is human nature, I know, but I want to be different. I am Your daughter. Let me shine, and when others ask me, "Why the smile?" or "Why the good deeds?" let me point them to You. You are the Source of all that is good in me. You have given me each ability I have. May I reflect Your love through my good works. Amen.*

Always point others to your heavenly Father when they notice you. There is nothing good in you without Him.

*Let your light so shine before men, that they may see your good works, and glorify your Father which is in heaven.*
MATTHEW 5:16

# Honoring My Parents

*Heavenly Father, show me how to honor my parents. Even as I have grown into a woman, Your command remains. Give me patience with my parents. Remind me that with age comes wisdom. Help me to seek their counsel when it is appropriate. God, in Your sovereignty, You gave me the mother and father that You did. May I honor You as I honor them. Amen.*

Honoring your parents looks different at four, fourteen, and forty, but this is a lifelong duty and privilege. God is pleased when you honor those who have filled parental roles in your life.

..............................................................................................................................

..............................................................................................................................

..............................................................................................................................

..............................................................................................................................

..............................................................................................................................

..............................................................................................................................

..............................................................................................................................

..............................................................................................................................

..............................................................................................................................

..............................................................................................................................

..............................................................................................................................

..............................................................................................................................

..............................................................................................................................

*Honour thy father and thy mother, as the LORD thy God hath commanded thee; that thy days may be prolonged, and that it may go well with thee, in the land which the LORD thy God giveth thee.*
DEUTERONOMY 5:16

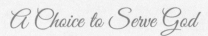

# A Choice to Serve God

*Father, it is a daily choice. Will I serve the world? Myself? Or my God?*
*What will I model for the children in my life who look up to me?*
*Will my family and friends know me as one who is self-serving or*
*kingdom-focused? Today I make the choice to serve the Lord.*
*Help me to truly live as Your servant in this world. Amen.*

As a woman, the choices you make often impact your entire
family. Choose to serve the Lord, that your influence might be
godly rather than worldly.

...................................................................................................................
...................................................................................................................
...................................................................................................................
...................................................................................................................
...................................................................................................................
...................................................................................................................
...................................................................................................................
...................................................................................................................
...................................................................................................................
...................................................................................................................
...................................................................................................................
...................................................................................................................
...................................................................................................................
...................................................................................................................
...................................................................................................................
...................................................................................................................

*As for me and my house, we will serve the LORD.*
JOSHUA 24:15

# Avoiding Idleness

*Lord, I know that You want me to take care of my household. Sometimes I am so tempted to put off my duties around the house, and I find myself spending too much time on the computer or the telephone. Help me to be balanced. Help me to take care of my household and to be aware of the trap of idleness. I know that procrastination is not a good or godly habit. Amen.*

Certainly every woman needs some downtime and relaxation, but do not confuse this with idleness. Idleness is a tool of the devil.

........................................................................................................

........................................................................................................

........................................................................................................

........................................................................................................

........................................................................................................

........................................................................................................

........................................................................................................

........................................................................................................

........................................................................................................

........................................................................................................

........................................................................................................

........................................................................................................

........................................................................................................

........................................................................................................

*She looketh well to the ways of her household,*
*and eateth not the bread of idleness.*
PROVERBS 31:27

# Every Good Gift

*Father, thank You for the blessings You have poured out on my family.
Often I dwell on that which we do not have. Please remind me to be ever
grateful for so many gifts. The comforts we enjoy each day like running
water and electricity are so easily taken for granted. Thank You for
Your provision in our lives. Help me to have a thankful heart so
that my family might be more thankful also. Amen.*

Sometimes making a list of all the things you are thankful for is
a good way to count your blessings. How has God blessed your
family?

.................................................................................................................................

.................................................................................................................................

.................................................................................................................................

.................................................................................................................................

.................................................................................................................................

.................................................................................................................................

.................................................................................................................................

.................................................................................................................................

.................................................................................................................................

.................................................................................................................................

.................................................................................................................................

.................................................................................................................................

.................................................................................................................................

.................................................................................................................................

*And thou shalt rejoice in every good thing which the
Lord thy God hath given unto thee, and unto thine house,
thou, and the Levite, and the stranger that is among you.*
DEUTERONOMY 26:11

# A God-Centered Home

*Father, so many homes are shaken in these days. So many families are shattering to pieces around me. Protect my home, I pray. Protect my loved ones. Be the foundation of my home, strong and solid, consistent and wise. May every decision made here reflect Your principles. May those who visit this home and encounter this family be keenly aware of our uniqueness, because we serve the one true and almighty God. Amen.*

If God is the center of your home, there will be much prayer there, and He will be considered in all of your family's decisions.

......................................................................................................................

......................................................................................................................

......................................................................................................................

......................................................................................................................

......................................................................................................................

......................................................................................................................

......................................................................................................................

......................................................................................................................

......................................................................................................................

......................................................................................................................

......................................................................................................................

......................................................................................................................

......................................................................................................................

......................................................................................................................

*Except the LORD build the house, they labour in vain that build it: except the LORD keep the city, the watchman waketh but in vain.*
PSALM 127:1

# A Godly Example

*God, help me to be an example of a faithful disciple of Christ to my family and friends. Those who are close in our lives have the ability to lead us toward or away from righteousness and godliness. I pray that all I do and say will honor You and that I will never be a stumbling block to others. May all within my sphere of influence find me faithful to You. Amen.*

Simply by your position and your role, you have influence. Use it wisely. Be a godly influence on those who watch your life.

........................................................................................................

........................................................................................................

........................................................................................................

........................................................................................................

........................................................................................................

........................................................................................................

........................................................................................................

........................................................................................................

........................................................................................................

........................................................................................................

........................................................................................................

........................................................................................................

........................................................................................................

........................................................................................................

*The righteous is more excellent than his neighbour: but the way of the wicked seduceth them.*
PROVERBS 12:26

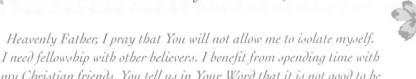

# The Value of Fellowship

*Heavenly Father, I pray that You will not allow me to isolate myself.
I need fellowship with other believers. I benefit from spending time with
my Christian friends. You tell us in Your Word that it is not good to be
alone. We need one another as we walk through this life with all of its
ups and downs. When I am tempted to distance myself from others,
guide me back into Christian fellowship. Amen.*

Are you in need of a Christian friend? Take steps to finding
one. Joining a Bible study group at a local church is a good
way to meet other women who are seeking God.

*Two are better than one; because they have a good reward
for their labour. For if they fall, the one will lift up his
fellow: but woe to him that is alone when he falleth;
for he hath not another to help him up.*
ECCLESIASTES 4:9–10

# Iron Sharpens Iron

*Lord, I find it hard to talk to my friends about areas of their lives in which they are not honoring You. And I certainly do not always appreciate their correction in my life! Father, allow such sweet, godly fellowship between my Christian sisters and me that when truth should be spoken in love, we are able to speak into one another's lives. We need one another. Iron sharpens iron. Amen.*

Choose the moment wisely if you feel led to share truth in love with a friend. Pray beforehand. Be sure that it is God leading you and not your own pride or opinions.

........................................................................................................................

........................................................................................................................

........................................................................................................................

........................................................................................................................

........................................................................................................................

........................................................................................................................

........................................................................................................................

........................................................................................................................

........................................................................................................................

........................................................................................................................

........................................................................................................................

........................................................................................................................

*Iron sharpeneth iron; so a man*
*sharpeneth the countenance of his friend.*
PROVERBS 27:17

# Resisting the Urge to Gossip

*Father, men don't seem to struggle with gossip the way we ladies do. A juicy tidbit of information is so tempting! I need Your help, Lord, to resist the temptation to gossip. Your Word warns me of the dangers of gossip and slander. Strengthen me so that I will not be a troublemaker but rather a peacemaker. Help me to resist the urge to listen to or speak gossip. Amen.*

God still considers gossip to be gossip when it is cloaked in phrases such as "I probably shouldn't say this" and "Bless her heart."

*A froward man soweth strife:
and a whisperer separateth chief friends.*
PROVERBS 16:28

# Shield of Faith

*God, guard my heart and mind with the shield of faith. I will call on the name of Jesus when Satan tempts me. I will fight against his schemes to ruin me. My weapon is my knowledge of Your Word, promises memorized and cherished. My defense is my faith in Jesus Christ, my Savior. On this faith I will stand. Increase my faith and protect me from the evil one, I pray. Amen.*

Satan is alive and well, but he cannot defeat those whose faith in Christ is solid and sure. He is helpless against it.

........................................................................................................
........................................................................................................
........................................................................................................
........................................................................................................
........................................................................................................
........................................................................................................
........................................................................................................
........................................................................................................
........................................................................................................
........................................................................................................
........................................................................................................
........................................................................................................
........................................................................................................
........................................................................................................

*Above all, taking the shield of faith, wherewith ye shall be able to quench all the fiery darts of the wicked.*
EPHESIANS 6:16

# Trust in the Lord

*Father, I lean on my own understanding, don't I? Help me to trust that You know what is best. Often I make plans and attempt to figure things out when I should submit it all to You in prayer. Bring to mind, as I sit quietly before You now, the times in the past when You have come through for me. Give me faith for my future, knowing that it is in my Father's hands. Amen.*

You will never regret putting God first. Lean into His goodness. He wants to bless you with good gifts. He is your loving Father.

......................................................................................................

......................................................................................................

......................................................................................................

......................................................................................................

......................................................................................................

......................................................................................................

......................................................................................................

......................................................................................................

......................................................................................................

......................................................................................................

......................................................................................................

......................................................................................................

*Trust in the LORD with all thine heart; and lean not unto thine own understanding. In all thy ways acknowledge him, and he shall direct thy paths.*
PROVERBS 3:5–6

# Things Not Seen

*Jesus, it is easy to believe in that which I can see. I wish I could reach out and touch You. As I meditate on Your Word, give me faith in that which I cannot see. Give me faith that all of Your promises are true and that one day You will come again in the clouds to take me home. Amen.*

Wait for Jesus like a child waits for Christmas. Wait for His second coming expectantly, with faith in what you have not seen.

........................................................................................................
........................................................................................................
........................................................................................................
........................................................................................................
........................................................................................................
........................................................................................................
........................................................................................................
........................................................................................................
........................................................................................................
........................................................................................................
........................................................................................................
........................................................................................................
........................................................................................................
........................................................................................................
........................................................................................................

*Now faith is the substance of things hoped for,*
*the evidence of things not seen.*
HEBREWS 11:1

# God Is Faithful

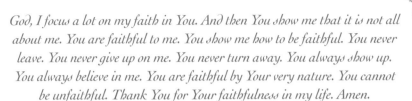

*God, I focus a lot on my faith in You. And then You show me that it is not all about me. You are faithful to me. You show me how to be faithful. You never leave. You never give up on me. You never turn away. You always show up. You always believe in me. You are faithful by Your very nature. You cannot be unfaithful. Thank You for Your faithfulness in my life. Amen.*

God is faithful. Period. Man may let you down, but you can count wholeheartedly on the faithfulness of your holy, loving God.

........................................................................................................................

........................................................................................................................

........................................................................................................................

........................................................................................................................

........................................................................................................................

........................................................................................................................

........................................................................................................................

........................................................................................................................

........................................................................................................................

........................................................................................................................

........................................................................................................................

........................................................................................................................

........................................................................................................................

........................................................................................................................

........................................................................................................................

*But the Lord is faithful, who shall stablish you,
and keep you from evil.*
2 THESSALONIANS 3:3

# Increase My Faith

*Lord, my faith is small. Thank You for the promise in Your Word that You can work with even a mustard seed of faith! I submit my lack of faith to You and ask that You grow and stretch my trust in You. I want my faith to be great. As I meditate on Your love for me, please increase my faith that You are sovereign and You will take care of all my needs. Amen.*

There are many things that man cannot attain, but nothing is impossible with God. That is why we need faith.

.............................................................................................

.............................................................................................

.............................................................................................

.............................................................................................

.............................................................................................

.............................................................................................

.............................................................................................

.............................................................................................

.............................................................................................

.............................................................................................

.............................................................................................

.............................................................................................

*Verily I say unto you, If ye have faith as a grain
of mustard seed, ye shall say unto this mountain,
Remove hence to yonder place; and it shall remove;
and nothing shall be impossible unto you.*
MATTHEW 17:20

# *Saved by Grace through Faith*

*God, it is so comforting to know that my position before You is secure. Thank You for seeing me through a new lens. When You look at me, because I have been saved through faith, You see Your Son in me. You no longer see sin but righteousness. I couldn't have earned it, no matter how hard I worked. Thank You for the gift of salvation through my faith in Jesus. Amen.*

A caterpillar, once it becomes a butterfly, can never go back to being a caterpillar. A Christian's position before God is secure upon the profession of faith in Christ.

.................................................................................................................
.................................................................................................................
.................................................................................................................
.................................................................................................................
.................................................................................................................
.................................................................................................................
.................................................................................................................
.................................................................................................................
.................................................................................................................
.................................................................................................................
.................................................................................................................
.................................................................................................................

*For by grace are ye saved through faith;
and that not of yourselves: it is the gift of God:
Not of works, lest any man should boast.*
EPHESIANS 2:8–9

# Faith Pleases God

*Father, I read of Enoch, Noah, Abraham, and Joseph. I know the stories of Sarah and Rahab. The Bible is full of men and women of faith. Those who pleased You were not those who were the wealthiest, most beautiful, or had the most important names. What pleases You, my Father, is faith. Without it, I cannot please You. I choose to live by faith as my spiritual ancestors lived. Strengthen my faith, I ask. Amen.*

To know that one cannot please God without faith inspires us to nurture and work out our faith. It is not a thing to be set upon the shelf and forgotten. It must be active and alive.

*But without faith it is impossible to please him:
for he that cometh to God must believe that he is,
and that he is a rewarder of them that diligently seek him.*
HEBREWS 11:6

# What Is My "Isaac"?

*Heavenly Father, I am amazed by the faith of Abraham. He offered up his son, Isaac, the one for whom he had waited and waited, the promised one. When You tested his faith, he answered immediately. He rose up early in the morning and acted on Your command. Would I have had the faith that Abraham had in You? Would I trust You even in my worst nightmare? I hope so. How I hope so. Amen.*

What is the Isaac in your life? What would be the most difficult thing for you to give up if God were to ask for it? Is it your job? A relationship? Consider your Isaac today.

..................................................................................................
..................................................................................................
..................................................................................................
..................................................................................................
..................................................................................................
..................................................................................................
..................................................................................................
..................................................................................................
..................................................................................................
..................................................................................................
..................................................................................................

*By faith Abraham, when he was tried, offered up Isaac: and he that had received the promises offered up his only begotten son, Of whom it was said, That in Isaac shall thy seed be called: Accounting that God was able to raise him up, even from the dead; from whence also he received him in a figure.*
HEBREWS 11:17–19

## Praying for Bold Faith

*I desire a bold faith, Jesus. Like the woman who followed You,*
*crying out, asking that You cast a demon from her daughter.*
*She was a Gentile, not a Jew; yet, she called You the "Son of David."*
*She acknowledged You as the Messiah. And You stopped. Her faith*
*impressed You. You healed the child. May I be so bold. May I recognize*
*that You are the only solution to every problem. Amen.*

Don't be afraid to go before the throne of God with confidence.
You are His child, saved by the blood of His Son. Have a bold
faith!

...........................................................................................................

...........................................................................................................

...........................................................................................................

...........................................................................................................

...........................................................................................................

...........................................................................................................

...........................................................................................................

...........................................................................................................

...........................................................................................................

...........................................................................................................

...........................................................................................................

...........................................................................................................

*Then Jesus answered and said unto her, O woman,*
*great is thy faith: be it unto thee even as thou wilt.*
*And her daughter was made whole from that very hour.*
MATTHEW 15:28

## *Trying of My Faith*

*Father, Your Word tells me that You have begun a good work in me and*
*You will be faithful to complete it. Help me to resist the temptation to*
*sin. I know that it's a process and that no one is perfect, but I desire*
*to grow in my faith. I want to be a faithful daughter of the King.*
*Bless my efforts, Father, and strengthen me as only You can. Amen.*

Do you count it as joy when temptations come? That is a tough
order. The Lord knows that your faith will not be complete and
perfect without trials. Stand firm.

................................................................................................................................

................................................................................................................................

................................................................................................................................

................................................................................................................................

................................................................................................................................

................................................................................................................................

................................................................................................................................

................................................................................................................................

................................................................................................................................

................................................................................................................................

................................................................................................................................

................................................................................................................................

*My brethren, count it all joy when ye fall into divers temptations;*
*Knowing this, that the trying of your faith worketh patience.*
*But let patience have her perfect work, that ye may be*
*perfect and entire, wanting nothing.*
JAMES 1:2–4

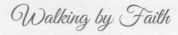

# Walking by Faith

*God, one day my faith shall be sight. In this life, I am called to walk by faith. In the next, I will see that which I have believed in for all these years. Earth is for faith, and heaven is for sight. Continue to nurture in me a deep faith, one that causes me to take each step of this journey with You as my focus. I walk by faith, not by sight. Amen.*

In an instant, this earthly body will be transformed. Everything will change. The greatest mountaintop-faith moments of this life will pale in comparison to even one moment of sight in heaven.

.................................................................................................................
.................................................................................................................
.................................................................................................................
.................................................................................................................
.................................................................................................................
.................................................................................................................
.................................................................................................................
.................................................................................................................
.................................................................................................................
.................................................................................................................
.................................................................................................................
.................................................................................................................
.................................................................................................................
.................................................................................................................
.................................................................................................................
.................................................................................................................

*For we walk by faith, not by sight.*
2 CORINTHIANS 5:7

# Resting on the Sabbath

*Father, You created us as beings that work and need rest. Sometimes I forget that. I get so caught up in all that must be accomplished. Slow my pace, Lord. Help me to honor You by resting one day per week. Help me to keep the Sabbath holy. Thank You for designing the week and for telling Your people to rest. It is up to me to follow Your command. Amen.*

Do you keep the Sabbath holy? Do you conduct business? Swing by the office? Tackle that mound of laundry? Or do you set aside the whole day to honor God and to rest?

........................................................................................................

........................................................................................................

........................................................................................................

........................................................................................................

........................................................................................................

........................................................................................................

........................................................................................................

........................................................................................................

........................................................................................................

........................................................................................................

........................................................................................................

........................................................................................................

*Remember the sabbath day, to keep it holy. Six days shalt thou labour, and do all thy work: But the seventh day is the sabbath of the LORD thy God: in it thou shalt not do any work.*
EXODUS 20:8–10

# Rest in the Lord

*Heavenly Father, take my worries and burdens. I submit to You my anxieties. Fill me with the rest that calms my spirit when I trust in You. Sometimes I look at others' lives and compare them to my own. Why do they have what I desire? Especially when I know that they are not Christians! But You tell me not to be concerned with others' prosperity. I choose to rest in You. Amen.*

Leave judgment to the Lord. He knows the hearts of men and women. Choose to rest in Jesus and to submit your requests to Him. He will take care of things.

.............................................................................................................................

.............................................................................................................................

.............................................................................................................................

.............................................................................................................................

.............................................................................................................................

.............................................................................................................................

.............................................................................................................................

.............................................................................................................................

.............................................................................................................................

.............................................................................................................................

.............................................................................................................................

.............................................................................................................................

*Rest in the Lord, and wait patiently for him:*
*fret not thyself because of him who prospereth in his way,*
*because of the man who bringeth wicked devices to pass.*
PSALM 37:7

# Invitation to Rest

*Jesus, You told Your disciples to rest. You directed them to leave the crowd and to relax and eat. You saw that they had been busy with ministry and they needed to recuperate. If You directed them to rest, even these twelve who worked at Your side daily, You must want me to rest as well. Remind me to take breaks from ministry. I needed to hear that You give me permission to rest! Amen.*

Legalism says to sign up for this, that, and the other ministry. It calls you to work beyond what Jesus desires. Listen to the Lord. He invites you to rest.

...................................................................................................................

...................................................................................................................

...................................................................................................................

...................................................................................................................

...................................................................................................................

...................................................................................................................

...................................................................................................................

...................................................................................................................

...................................................................................................................

...................................................................................................................

...................................................................................................................

...................................................................................................................

*And he said unto them, Come ye yourselves apart into a desert place, and rest a while: for there were many coming and going, and they had no leisure so much as to eat.*
MARK 6:31

*Father, as I am still before You this morning, I focus on who You are. You are sovereign, all-knowing, and You have plans to prosper and not to harm me. You are the Prince of Peace, my provider, my protector, and my friend. You are holy and yet You draw near to me when I draw near to You. You are the one true God. And I worship You in the quiet of this morning. Amen.*

There is a reason that scripture says to *be still*. Our minds and bodies need to be still before Him in order to focus on who God is.

........................................................................................................

........................................................................................................

........................................................................................................

........................................................................................................

........................................................................................................

........................................................................................................

........................................................................................................

........................................................................................................

........................................................................................................

........................................................................................................

........................................................................................................

........................................................................................................

........................................................................................................

*Be still, and know that I am God: I will be exalted among the heathen, I will be exalted in the earth.*
PSALM 46:10

# Calming the Storms

*Lord, sometimes You calm storms, and other times You carry
Your children through them. There is a storm raging in my heart.
I ask that You end it, but I desire Your will for my life. If I must
walk through this storm, will You go with me every step of the way?
You are where my heart finds rest and peace, regardless of the
outward circumstances. I love You, Lord. Amen.*

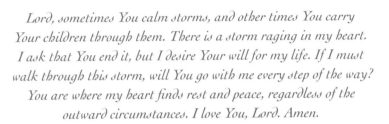

Wouldn't it have been amazing to witness Jesus calming the
storm from the boat that day? What storms has He calmed in
your life?

..................................................................................................................

..................................................................................................................

..................................................................................................................

..................................................................................................................

..................................................................................................................

..................................................................................................................

..................................................................................................................

..................................................................................................................

..................................................................................................................

..................................................................................................................

..................................................................................................................

..................................................................................................................

*And he arose, and rebuked the wind, and said unto the sea, Peace, be still.
And the wind ceased, and there was a great calm.*
MARK 4:39

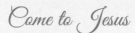

# Come to Jesus

*I come to You, Lord Jesus. That is the first step. I come before You now in this quiet moment. As I begin this new day, calm my spirit. There is work that must be done today. But even as I work, I can find rest in You. Ease the tension and stress in me, Lord, as only You can do. Thank You for a sense of peace. Amen.*

Do you sometimes feel that you can't carry the load you've been given? Turn it over to Jesus. Don't carry that which you were not meant to bear.

*Come unto me, all ye that labour and are heavy laden, and I will give you rest.*
MATTHEW 11:28

# Relaxation

*Thank You, God, for the gift of relaxation. It is so nice to sit out on a patio in springtime or by the fireplace in winter and enjoy a good meal with friends or family. It is relaxing to my mind, my heart, and my spirit. Help me to always set aside time to fellowship with others and to relax. Thank You for this blessing. Amen.*

Jesus ate and drank with His disciples. He visited the homes of all sorts of people and enjoyed meals with them. Just as Jesus modeled service, He also demonstrated relaxation.

..................................................................................................................................

..................................................................................................................................

..................................................................................................................................

..................................................................................................................................

..................................................................................................................................

..................................................................................................................................

..................................................................................................................................

..................................................................................................................................

..................................................................................................................................

..................................................................................................................................

..................................................................................................................................

..................................................................................................................................

*There is nothing better for a man, than that he should eat and drink, and that he should make his soul enjoy good in his labour. This also I saw, that it was from the hand of God. For who can eat, or who else can hasten hereunto, more than I?*
Ecclesiastes 2:24–25

# Finding Balance

*Jesus, when I think of Your ministry here on earth, I picture You teaching and casting out demons. You fed the five thousand and conversed with the woman at the well. You raised Lazarus from the dead! What a flurry of activity! But then I read that You slept. . .and during a storm that was frightening Your friends. If You rested, so shall I. I will set aside my work when it is appropriate to rest. Amen.*

Some people do nothing but work. Others are lazy. Jesus desires a balanced life for you. Work and play are both good for you. Establish balance between the two.

.........................................................................................................................
.........................................................................................................................
.........................................................................................................................
.........................................................................................................................
.........................................................................................................................
.........................................................................................................................
.........................................................................................................................
.........................................................................................................................
.........................................................................................................................
.........................................................................................................................
.........................................................................................................................
.........................................................................................................................

*And, behold, there arose a great tempest in the sea, insomuch that the ship was covered with the waves: but he was asleep.*
MATTHEW 8:24

# Peaceful Sleep

*Father, thank You for the refreshment that sleep provides. I know it is Your desire that I rest after working all day. I will not fear the darkness of the night. I have nothing to be afraid of because You watch over me. Thank You for sweet, peaceful sleep. As I go about my day today, give me energy for the tasks at hand. And when evening comes, grant me rest again, I pray. Amen.*

Make the closing activity of the day a conversation with God. Talking with your heavenly Father and casting your cares on Him will help you to rest easy through the night.

..................................................................................................
..................................................................................................
..................................................................................................
..................................................................................................
..................................................................................................
..................................................................................................
..................................................................................................
..................................................................................................
..................................................................................................
..................................................................................................
..................................................................................................
..................................................................................................
..................................................................................................

*When thou liest down, thou shalt not be afraid:
yea, thou shalt lie down, and thy sleep shall be sweet.*
PROVERBS 3:24

# Patience in a Busy World

*Father, patience isn't easy. This is a busy, fast-paced world in which
I exist! I drive through fast-food restaurant windows and receive hot
food within a few minutes. Automated bank tellers provide cash in an
instant. There is not much I have to wait for in this modern age.
But I realize that some of the things that matter most require great
patience. Teach me to wait with grace. Amen.*

If you are waiting for something you desire, trust God. The
Bible promises that He will not withhold any good and perfect
gift from His children.

........................................................................................................

........................................................................................................

........................................................................................................

........................................................................................................

........................................................................................................

........................................................................................................

........................................................................................................

........................................................................................................

........................................................................................................

........................................................................................................

........................................................................................................

........................................................................................................

*Now we exhort you, brethren, warn them that are unruly, comfort the
feebleminded, support the weak, be patient toward all men.*
1 Thessalonians 5:14

## Waiting for Christ's Return

*Lord Jesus, the evening news reports are full of sadness. At times,
I wonder why You are waiting. Why don't You come back for Your
people? Why don't You take us out of this world full of sin and pain?
I know there is a better place, another life waiting for us in heaven.
Give me patience. No one knows the day that You will return.
As I wait, may I keep my eyes fixed on You. Amen.*

The media seems to focus on reporting on the negative. Try
writing in a "thankful journal" each morning as you begin your
day. What are you thankful for?

........................................................................................................

........................................................................................................

........................................................................................................

........................................................................................................

........................................................................................................

........................................................................................................

........................................................................................................

........................................................................................................

........................................................................................................

........................................................................................................

........................................................................................................

*Be patient therefore, brethren, unto the coming of the Lord. Behold,
the husbandman waiteth for the precious fruit of the earth, and hath
long patience for it, until he receive the early and latter rain. Be ye also
patient; stablish your hearts: for the coming of the Lord draweth nigh.*
JAMES 5:7–8

# Slow to Speak

*Father, I am often the opposite of what James advises in these verses. I catch myself being quick to speak and slow to listen. I make assumptions and find out later I was wrong. I say things and later wish I had gotten all the facts first. Lord, I admit that this is not an easy task—being patient with those around me. Please put a guard over my tongue. Amen.*

The first step to change is admitting there is a problem. If you want to be quicker to listen and slower to speak, admit that it is tough. . .and then try to do better. God will bless your efforts.

..................................................................................................

..................................................................................................

..................................................................................................

..................................................................................................

..................................................................................................

..................................................................................................

..................................................................................................

..................................................................................................

..................................................................................................

..................................................................................................

..................................................................................................

..................................................................................................

..................................................................................................

*Wherefore, my beloved brethren, let every man be swift to hear, slow to speak, slow to wrath: For the wrath of man worketh not the righteousness of God.*
JAMES 1:19–20

## Patient but Not Lazy

*Jesus, there is so much work to be done. There are so many who have not heard the good news of Christ yet! As Your people, we must be about kingdom work and spreading the Gospel. You have given us the great commission to go into the world and tell others. But we must also be patient in our faith as we await the perfect timing of Your second coming! Amen.*

There is a time for everything. In Ecclesiastes, we are told that there is a time to work and a time to rest. Be patient but not lazy.

............................................................................................
............................................................................................
............................................................................................
............................................................................................
............................................................................................
............................................................................................
............................................................................................
............................................................................................
............................................................................................
............................................................................................
............................................................................................
............................................................................................
............................................................................................
............................................................................................
............................................................................................
............................................................................................

*That ye be not slothful, but followers of them*
*who through faith and patience inherit the promises.*
HEBREWS 6:12

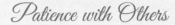

## Patience with Others

*Father, make me a little more like Jesus each day. Make me sensitive to the Holy Spirit when I am tempted to be impatient. Let me be known as one who is kind, merciful, and humble. When others describe me, I am not sure they would use these adjectives. Just as You bear with me, help me to bear with my family, friends, and colleagues with a spirit of forgiveness. Amen.*

God has forgiven you. Forgive others. God has been patient with you. Be patient with others.

...........................................................................................................................

...........................................................................................................................

...........................................................................................................................

...........................................................................................................................

...........................................................................................................................

...........................................................................................................................

...........................................................................................................................

...........................................................................................................................

...........................................................................................................................

...........................................................................................................................

...........................................................................................................................

...........................................................................................................................

*Put on therefore, as the elect of God, holy and beloved, bowels of mercies, kindness, humbleness of mind, meekness, longsuffering; Forbearing one another, and forgiving one another, if any man have a quarrel against any: even as Christ forgave you, so also do ye.*
COLOSSIANS 3:12–13

## Slow to Anger

*Lord, like a virus, a spirit of dissatisfaction spreads quickly. It can infect everyone who comes near. You warn me in Your Word about this. You want Your people to be slow to anger. Help me to be aware of the impact my attitude and my reactions have on those within my sphere of influence. I truly want to be a peacemaker and not one who is known for stirring up trouble. Amen.*

Jesus expressed anger during His ministry on earth, but if you study the Bible, you will see that it was always a godly wrath over offenses to the Father.

...................................................................................................

...................................................................................................

...................................................................................................

...................................................................................................

...................................................................................................

...................................................................................................

...................................................................................................

...................................................................................................

...................................................................................................

...................................................................................................

...................................................................................................

...................................................................................................

*A wrathful man stirreth up strife:*
*but he that is slow to anger appeaseth strife.*
PROVERBS 15:18

# Following Christ's Example

*Lord, You are always there, and You are consistently patient with me. What if it were not so? What if You reached Your limit and showed the wrath that I deserve in my sinful imperfection? Because of Your great patience with me, let me not grow tired of being patient myself. Let me model what You have shown me by Your example. Thank You for Your great patience with me, God. Amen.*

Anything that Jesus asks of us, He models well. Get to know the Savior through prayer and the reading of His Word, and His character traits will become apparent in you.

........................................................................................................................

........................................................................................................................

........................................................................................................................

........................................................................................................................

........................................................................................................................

........................................................................................................................

........................................................................................................................

........................................................................................................................

........................................................................................................................

........................................................................................................................

........................................................................................................................

........................................................................................................................

........................................................................................................................

........................................................................................................................

*And let us not be weary in well doing:
for in due season we shall reap, if we faint not.*
GALATIANS 6:9

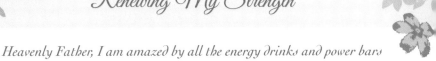

# Renewing My Strength

*Heavenly Father, I am amazed by all the energy drinks and power bars available these days at the grocery store. If only everyone could see that true strength, true energy comes from You! Certainly exercise and good nutrition are helpful. But inner strength, the type that endures life's hardships and trials, is found only in a relationship with Christ. I am so thankful I have this great source of strength. Amen.*

Patience develops perseverance. If you want to finish the race well, learn to wait patiently upon the Lord.

........................................................................................................................

........................................................................................................................

........................................................................................................................

........................................................................................................................

........................................................................................................................

........................................................................................................................

........................................................................................................................

........................................................................................................................

........................................................................................................................

........................................................................................................................

........................................................................................................................

........................................................................................................................

........................................................................................................................

*But they that wait upon the LORD shall renew their strength; they shall mount up with wings as eagles; they shall run, and not be weary; and they shall walk, and not faint.*
ISAIAH 40:31

# Patience and Wisdom

*Father, patience and wisdom seem to go hand in hand. I am beginning to determine that the wisest people I know are also some of the most patient. They seek You in every trial. They exhibit Your character traits. Give me patience. Help me to be still before You and to seek You in my life. May I grow in wisdom through being patient as You teach and stretch me. Amen.*

If you want to be wise, read God's Word. Take your time with it. Ask God to instruct you and change you through His Word. Patience is a key to wisdom.

........................................................................................................

........................................................................................................

........................................................................................................

........................................................................................................

........................................................................................................

........................................................................................................

........................................................................................................

........................................................................................................

........................................................................................................

........................................................................................................

........................................................................................................

........................................................................................................

........................................................................................................

*But the wisdom that is from above is first pure, then peaceable, gentle, and easy to be intreated, full of mercy and good fruits, without partiality, and without hypocrisy.*
JAMES 3:17

# In Christ's Strength

*Father, I am so thankful for the strength that is mine as a Christian.*
*I cannot do anything on my own, but through Christ, I can do all things.*
*It is comforting to know that the word all includes the trials and concerns*
*that I bring to You this morning. I lay them at Your feet, Lord. I take You*
*at Your Word. I can do all things through Jesus, who lives in me. Amen.*

Recognizing that it is Christ who strengthens you takes some of
the pressure off. You can't do it on your own. Focus instead on
your strength through Him!

........................................................................................................................

........................................................................................................................

........................................................................................................................

........................................................................................................................

........................................................................................................................

........................................................................................................................

........................................................................................................................

........................................................................................................................

........................................................................................................................

........................................................................................................................

........................................................................................................................

........................................................................................................................

........................................................................................................................

........................................................................................................................

*I can do all things through Christ which strengtheneth me.*
PHILIPPIANS 4:13

# Strength to Combat Temptation

*God, at times I sink so deep into temptation that I forget Your promise. You have said that there is always a way out, a way of escape. You have promised in Your Word that nothing is strong enough to separate me from Your love. I confess to You this morning that temptation is alive and well in my heart. Set my eyes on the way of escape. Free me from temptation, I pray. Amen.*

Whatever the temptation that pulls at your heartstrings, Jesus is stronger. Jesus is for you and never against you. He has provided an exit sign. Flee temptation to sin.

........................................................................................................................

........................................................................................................................

........................................................................................................................

........................................................................................................................

........................................................................................................................

........................................................................................................................

........................................................................................................................

........................................................................................................................

........................................................................................................................

........................................................................................................................

........................................................................................................................

*There hath no temptation taken you but such as is common to man:
but God is faithful, who will not suffer you to be tempted above
that ye are able; but will with the temptation also make a
way to escape, that ye may be able to bear it.*
1 CORINTHIANS 10:13

# My Source of Strength

*Father, at times I worry too much about what others think of me.*
*Even when I just have a minor disagreement with a friend or coworker,*
*I am afraid that the person will not like me anymore. I worry that I have not*
*lived up to what was expected of me. Remind me, Father, that I must seek my*
*ultimate strength and encouragement from You and You alone. Amen.*

Remember that your position before God has been established through Christ. It is secure. God sees you as His precious daughter. Find strength in this.

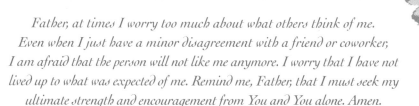

*And David was greatly distressed; for the people spake of stoning him,*
*because the soul of all the people was grieved, every man for his sons and*
*for his daughters: but David encouraged himself in the LORD his God.*
1 SAMUEL 30:6

# God Is with Me

*Heavenly Father, as I meet with You this morning, I find great strength in the knowledge that You will never leave me. Wherever I go, You are there with me. You are not just beside me, but You reside in my heart. I never have to be afraid. The Lord Almighty, the Maker of heaven and earth, is with me. Thank You, Father, for the strength I find in You. Amen.*

When life throws you a curveball and you are confused, remember that God is still with you. He will never leave you or forsake you.

.................................................................................................................

.................................................................................................................

.................................................................................................................

.................................................................................................................

.................................................................................................................

.................................................................................................................

.................................................................................................................

.................................................................................................................

.................................................................................................................

.................................................................................................................

.................................................................................................................

.................................................................................................................

.................................................................................................................

*Have not I commanded thee? Be strong and of a*
*good courage; be not afraid, neither be thou dismayed:*
*for the LORD thy God is with thee whithersoever thou goest.*
JOSHUA 1:9

# Mountain-Moving Faith

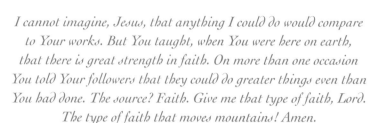

*I cannot imagine, Jesus, that anything I could do would compare to Your works. But You taught, when You were here on earth, that there is great strength in faith. On more than one occasion You told Your followers that they could do greater things even than You had done. The source? Faith. Give me that type of faith, Lord. The type of faith that moves mountains! Amen.*

Some days it may seem that your faith is small. Jesus said that there is great power in even faith the size of a tiny mustard seed.

.................................................................................................
.................................................................................................
.................................................................................................
.................................................................................................
.................................................................................................
.................................................................................................
.................................................................................................
.................................................................................................
.................................................................................................
.................................................................................................
.................................................................................................
.................................................................................................

*Jesus answered and said unto them, Verily I say unto you, If ye have faith, and doubt not, ye shall not only do this which is done to the fig tree, but also if ye shall say unto this mountain, Be thou removed, and be thou cast into the sea; it shall be done.*
Matthew 21:21

# Fear No Evil

*How wonderful, God, that death has no power over the Christian!*
*You are a strong and mighty God, the one true God. You are with me,*
*protecting me all the way. And when the end of this life comes,*
*whenever that may be, You will walk with me through the valley*
*of the shadow of death. Death has lost its sting because Christ*
*has conquered it! In Your name I pray, amen.*

There is great strength for the believer in Christ who faces
even a terminal illness. We will all die a physical death, but our
spirits will live for eternity with Jesus!

.............................................................................................................
.............................................................................................................
.............................................................................................................
.............................................................................................................
.............................................................................................................
.............................................................................................................
.............................................................................................................
.............................................................................................................
.............................................................................................................
.............................................................................................................
.............................................................................................................
.............................................................................................................

*Yea, though I walk through the valley of the shadow*
*of death, I will fear no evil: for thou art with me;*
*thy rod and thy staff they comfort me.*
PSALM 23:4

# A Spirit of Power

*God, a spirit of fear is not from You! It is from the enemy. I choose to believe the promise from Your Word that You have given believers a spirit of power, love, and a sound mind. I will go about my day with strength. I will love others well. I will make solid and right decisions based on Your living Word. I claim this promise. You are my strength! Amen.*

Messages that whisper what you *cannot* do are from the evil one. God's messages for you will always be concerning what you *can* do. Through Christ, you are able.

........................................................................................................................

........................................................................................................................

........................................................................................................................

........................................................................................................................

........................................................................................................................

........................................................................................................................

........................................................................................................................

........................................................................................................................

........................................................................................................................

........................................................................................................................

........................................................................................................................

........................................................................................................................

........................................................................................................................

........................................................................................................................

........................................................................................................................

*For God hath not given us the spirit of fear;
but of power, and of love, and of a sound mind.*
2 TIMOTHY 1:7

# My Strength and My Song

*Lord, You don't just provide my strength. You ARE my strength. Through You, I am able to do all things. At times I forget this. I lean on my own strength, which is never enough. It always fails me. Today I will stand firm on my foundation, which is salvation through Christ. I will find my strength in the one true God. I will worship You with my life. Amen.*

When unbelievers ask you how you are so strong when facing tough circumstances, always give the glory to God. He is glorified when you give Him credit for your strength.

........................................................................................

........................................................................................

........................................................................................

........................................................................................

........................................................................................

........................................................................................

........................................................................................

........................................................................................

........................................................................................

........................................................................................

........................................................................................

........................................................................................

*The Lord is my strength and song, and he is become my salvation:*
*he is my God, and I will prepare him an habitation;*
*my father's God, and I will exalt him.*
EXODUS 15:2

# Sharing the Good News

*Why do I find it so hard just to open my mouth and share the Gospel?*
*Give me strength, Lord, to share the good news of Jesus with others.*
*When the opportunity presents itself, even today, I ask that You will*
*give me strength to share openly. The world needs You. I have received*
*the Good News, and it is my responsibility to spread the word.*
*Empower me, I pray. In Your name, amen.*

The strength for sharing the Gospel with another must come
directly from Christ. At the very same time, the Holy Spirit
must miraculously draw the new believer unto Himself.

...........................................................................................................................

...........................................................................................................................

...........................................................................................................................

...........................................................................................................................

...........................................................................................................................

...........................................................................................................................

...........................................................................................................................

...........................................................................................................................

...........................................................................................................................

...........................................................................................................................

...........................................................................................................................

...........................................................................................................................

*Notwithstanding the Lord stood with me, and strengthened me; that by me*
*the preaching might be fully known, and that all the Gentiles might hear:*
*and I was delivered out of the mouth of the lion.*
2 TIMOTHY 4:17

# He Is Strong

*God, please show Yourself strong in my time of need! I need Your strength today. Just as the song says, "I am weak, but You are strong." I am so thankful for that exception today. "But You are strong." I will cling to that. When I am at my very weakest, when there seems to be no way I can face the future, I will face it in Your strength. Show Yourself strong in my life. In Jesus' name, amen.*

"Jesus loves me. This I know, for the Bible tells me so. Little ones to Him belong. They are weak, *but He is strong.*"

.................................................................................................................................
.................................................................................................................................
.................................................................................................................................
.................................................................................................................................
.................................................................................................................................
.................................................................................................................................
.................................................................................................................................
.................................................................................................................................
.................................................................................................................................
.................................................................................................................................
.................................................................................................................................
.................................................................................................................................
.................................................................................................................................

*For the eyes of the LORD run to and fro throughout the whole earth, to shew himself strong in the behalf of them whose heart is perfect toward him.*
2 CHRONICLES 16:9

# He Increases My Strength

*All I have ever known is this body, Father. All I know is becoming weary. This body grows weak at times. But You are different. You never grow tired. You don't sleep or look away. Your eye is always upon my life. Your strength is consistent and eternal. Renew my strength, Lord. I need physical and spiritual power to live in this world. Thank You for strengthening me! Amen.*

You are set apart because you belong to God. One day you will have a new body, a spiritual one that will never grow weary again.

....................................................................................................

....................................................................................................

....................................................................................................

....................................................................................................

....................................................................................................

....................................................................................................

....................................................................................................

....................................................................................................

....................................................................................................

....................................................................................................

....................................................................................................

*He giveth power to the faint; and to them that have no might he increaseth strength. Even the youths shall faint and be weary, and the young men shall utterly fall: But they that wait upon the LORD shall renew their strength; they shall mount up with wings as eagles; they shall run, and not be weary; and they shall walk, and not faint.*
ISAIAH 40:29–31

# Influencing Children

*Lord, let Your Word and Your ways season my conversations.
I am to be salt and light in the world. May I truly be such for those
who look up to me. I know there is great power in influence. Attitudes
and opinions are easily noted by children, who may be young but
are quick to pick up on adults' feelings. I pray that the subtleties
in my conversations and actions will honor You. Amen.*

Whether or not you are a mother, you influence the children in
your life. Children need to see Jesus in you.

..................................................................................................................................................................
..................................................................................................................................................................
..................................................................................................................................................................
..................................................................................................................................................................
..................................................................................................................................................................
..................................................................................................................................................................
..................................................................................................................................................................
..................................................................................................................................................................
..................................................................................................................................................................
..................................................................................................................................................................
..................................................................................................................................................................
..................................................................................................................................................................
..................................................................................................................................................................

*And these words, which I command thee this day, shall be in thine heart:
And thou shalt teach them diligently unto thy children, and shalt talk of
them when thou sittest in thine house, and when thou walkest by the way,
and when thou liest down, and when thou risest up.*

DEUTERONOMY 6:6–7

# Starting Where I Am

*Jesus, You give tall orders! How can I teach all nations and baptize people? Oh. . .You mean I might not even have to leave my community? There are people all around me who don't know You, Lord. Help me to start with those in my sphere of influence. The grocery store clerk who seems tired and distraught. . . The teacher at my child's school who is so lost. . . Give me the courage to reach out. Amen.*

Certainly the Lord calls us to the ends of the earth, but He is just as concerned with the soul of your neighbor. Start where you are.

......................................................................................................................
......................................................................................................................
......................................................................................................................
......................................................................................................................
......................................................................................................................
......................................................................................................................
......................................................................................................................
......................................................................................................................
......................................................................................................................
......................................................................................................................
......................................................................................................................
......................................................................................................................
......................................................................................................................

*Go ye therefore, and teach all nations, baptizing them in the name of the Father, and of the Son, and of the Holy Ghost.*
MATTHEW 28:19

# Unhealthy Influences

*God, please help me to know how to balance being in the world but not of it. You have blessed me with other believers to walk through life with and to receive counsel from when needed. I want to stay true to Your Word in how I live my life. I want my habits to reflect my faith. Please keep me from the power of influences that are not healthy for me. Amen.*

A bad habit does not start overnight. Often, it is a series of temptations or events that pull one into it. Be on guard against such influences.

.......................................................................................................
.......................................................................................................
.......................................................................................................
.......................................................................................................
.......................................................................................................
.......................................................................................................
.......................................................................................................
.......................................................................................................
.......................................................................................................
.......................................................................................................
.......................................................................................................
.......................................................................................................
.......................................................................................................
.......................................................................................................
.......................................................................................................

*Be not deceived: evil communications corrupt good manners.*
1 CORINTHIANS 15:33

# Integrity

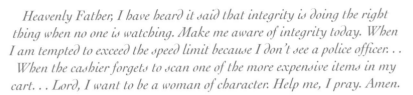

*Heavenly Father, I have heard it said that integrity is doing the right thing when no one is watching. Make me aware of integrity today. When I am tempted to exceed the speed limit because I don't see a police officer. . . When the cashier forgets to scan one of the more expensive items in my cart. . . Lord, I want to be a woman of character. Help me, I pray. Amen.*

You will never regret doing what is right. Often, even when you think no one is watching, someone is.

*Let integrity and uprightness preserve me; for I wait on thee.*
PSALM 25:21

# Influencing Family Members

*Lord, sometimes I am discouraged because certain family members don't seem interested in spiritual matters. They are living for the world and for the moment. I long for my immediate and extended family to know Jesus as their personal Savior. Give me the words to say when the time is right. Help me to remember that the way I live is a testimony before the lost as to how great You are. Amen.*

The way you handle crisis or disappointment will be watched by those who don't know Christ. They will notice the underlying peace you have, and they just may want it for themselves.

......................................................................................................................

......................................................................................................................

......................................................................................................................

......................................................................................................................

......................................................................................................................

......................................................................................................................

......................................................................................................................

......................................................................................................................

......................................................................................................................

......................................................................................................................

......................................................................................................................

*For the unbelieving husband is sanctified by the wife,
and the unbelieving wife is sanctified by the husband:
else were your children unclean; but now are they holy.*
1 Corinthians 7:14

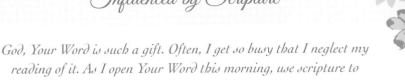

# Influenced by Scripture

*God, Your Word is such a gift. Often, I get so busy that I neglect my reading of it. As I open Your Word this morning, use scripture to influence my actions and reactions throughout this day. As I reflect on where I invest most of my time, help me to choose a time and place to read Your Word each day. What could be more important? Thank You for Your holy Word. Amen.*

God loves you so much that He has given you a guidebook for life. It is called the Bible. It is full of His great promises and also some warnings that Christians should heed.

........................................................................................................

........................................................................................................

........................................................................................................

........................................................................................................

........................................................................................................

........................................................................................................

........................................................................................................

........................................................................................................

........................................................................................................

........................................................................................................

*And that from a child thou hast known the holy scriptures, which are able to make thee wise unto salvation through faith which is in Christ Jesus. All scripture is given by inspiration of God, and is profitable for doctrine, for reproof, for correction, for instruction in righteousness.*
2 TIMOTHY 3:15–16

# Reflecting God's Love to Others

*Lord, I truly want to influence my little corner of the world for Christ. Sometimes I can relate to the persecution that the heroes of the Bible experienced. It stings when someone sarcastically says, "Pray for me!" Help me to remember that I should never be ashamed of my faith. Give me a kind spirit and a gentleness that reflects Your love, regardless of the circumstances. Amen.*

It's often easier just to go along with the crowd's way of thinking or doing; however, making godly choices will always serve you well.

.................................................................................................

.................................................................................................

.................................................................................................

.................................................................................................

.................................................................................................

.................................................................................................

.................................................................................................

.................................................................................................

.................................................................................................

.................................................................................................

.................................................................................................

.................................................................................................

*Having a good conscience; that, whereas they speak evil of you, as of evildoers, they may be ashamed that falsely accuse your good conversation in Christ.*
1 Peter 3:16

# Protection from Temptation

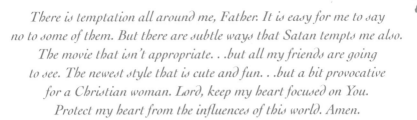

*There is temptation all around me, Father. It is easy for me to say
no to some of them. But there are subtle ways that Satan tempts me also.
The movie that isn't appropriate. . .but all my friends are going
to see. The newest style that is cute and fun. . .but a bit provocative
for a Christian woman. Lord, keep my heart focused on You.
Protect my heart from the influences of this world. Amen.*

The writer of Proverbs got it right on this one. Don't play
with fire, or you will get burned! Beware: Many of Satan's
temptations in our lives are subtle.

........................................................................................................

........................................................................................................

........................................................................................................

........................................................................................................

........................................................................................................

........................................................................................................

........................................................................................................

........................................................................................................

........................................................................................................

........................................................................................................

........................................................................................................

........................................................................................................

*Can a man take fire in his bosom,
and his clothes not be burned?*
PROVERBS 6:27

# Christian Friends

*Thank You, Lord, for Christian friends. They help me to stay true to You. They point me back to You when I stray. As I watch the way they face problems and hear them tell of Your steadfastness in their lives, I am encouraged. There is nothing like a sister in the Lord who comes alongside and says, "Let's do life together." Thank You, Father, for my believing friends' influence in my life. Amen.*

As Christians, we are in the world but not of it. Certainly, reach out to those who don't know Jesus! But those who speak into your life should walk with Christ.

........................................................................................................

........................................................................................................

........................................................................................................

........................................................................................................

........................................................................................................

........................................................................................................

........................................................................................................

........................................................................................................

........................................................................................................

........................................................................................................

........................................................................................................

........................................................................................................

........................................................................................................

*He that walketh with wise men shall be wise:*
*but a companion of fools shall be destroyed.*
Proverbs 13:20

## Serious Warning

*Everywhere I look, Father, my society says it's okay. Sex before marriage and outside of marriage. You warn us that this type of sin is of a serious nature. What we do with our bodies stays in our hearts and minds for a very long time. Protect me from the influences in my life that say these things are permissible when Your Word clearly states they are not good for me. Amen.*

The Bible does not just tell men and women to avoid fornication. It says to *flee* it! This is a serious warning from a serious God.

........................................................................................

........................................................................................

........................................................................................

........................................................................................

........................................................................................

........................................................................................

........................................................................................

........................................................................................

........................................................................................

........................................................................................

........................................................................................

........................................................................................

........................................................................................

*Flee fornication. Every sin that a man doeth is without the body; but he that committeth fornication sinneth against his own body.*
1 CORINTHIANS 6:18

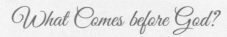

# What Comes before God?

*Graven images? Idols? Other gods? I don't struggle with this, Lord!*
*You are my God! But on second thought. . .I do. My idols don't look like*
*those of the Old Testament. But I have them. How do I spend my time?*
*My money? What could be taken from me that would devastate me?*
*Not even a relationship or my own children should come before You.*
*And certainly not shopping or the latest gadgets. Amen.*

What consumes most of your time and attention? Don't let anything come between you and the Lord. He wants to be number one in your life.

.................................................................................................................

.................................................................................................................

.................................................................................................................

.................................................................................................................

.................................................................................................................

.................................................................................................................

.................................................................................................................

.................................................................................................................

.................................................................................................................

.................................................................................................................

.................................................................................................................

*Thou shalt not bow down thyself to them, nor serve them:*
*for I the LORD thy God am a jealous God, visiting the*
*iniquity of the fathers upon the children unto the third*
*and fourth generation of them that hate me.*
EXODUS 20:5

## Confidence in the Lord

*Lord, I admit it. Sometimes I am afraid. I feel helpless. My mind runs wild with anxiety. Thank You for the promise that through Christ, this is not my norm. Certainly at times, in my humanity, I cower before an unknown future or feel defeated by the pressures of today. But You have given me a spirit of power and love. You have given me a sound mind. I find my confidence in You, God. Amen.*

Your heavenly Father has put His Holy Spirit in you to comfort you and guide you. Ask Him to do just that today. He will come through. . .every time!

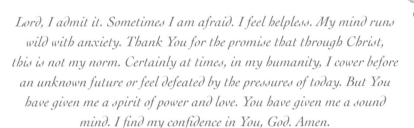

*For God hath not given us the spirit of fear;*
*but of power, and of love, and of a sound mind.*
2 TIMOTHY 1:7

# God Knows Me

*God, the Bible says that You knew me even before I was formed in my mother's womb. I find confidence in this. You have been with me all along this journey! As I face this day, help me to remember that I am never alone. You go before me to prepare the future. You walk with me through the present. And You were there with me since before I was born. Wow! Amen.*

When a child rides high upon her father's shoulders, she is the queen of the world! Find confidence in the fact that the God of the universe carries you today!

..................................................................................................................

..................................................................................................................

..................................................................................................................

..................................................................................................................

..................................................................................................................

..................................................................................................................

..................................................................................................................

..................................................................................................................

..................................................................................................................

..................................................................................................................

..................................................................................................................

..................................................................................................................

*For thou hast possessed my reins: thou hast covered me in my mother's womb. I will praise thee; for I am fearfully and wonderfully made: marvellous are thy works; and that my soul knoweth right well.*
PSALM 139:13–14

# Taking a Stand

*There is nothing in this world that can separate me from Your love!*
*Father, what strength I find in this promise! As a Christian,*
*I stand out. At times, no one agrees with the stand I take or the*
*choices I make. Sometimes it feels like the whole world is on the*
*other side! Thank You that You are always with me. I face this*
*day with confidence because You are on my side. Amen.*

We read of great men and women of God in the Bible who took a stand for Christ. Sometimes no one else supported them. But God was with them!

.................................................................................
.................................................................................
.................................................................................
.................................................................................
.................................................................................
.................................................................................
.................................................................................
.................................................................................
.................................................................................
.................................................................................
.................................................................................
.................................................................................
.................................................................................

*Though an host should encamp against me, my heart shall not fear:*
*though war should rise against me, in this will I be confident.*
Psalm 27:3

# Facing the Future

*Lord, thank You that I don't have to worry about tomorrow. I can face an uncertain future with a certain God at my side. You are all the confidence I need! You have never left me, and You never will. Tomorrow may bring a scary diagnosis, an unthinkable loss, or a deep disappointment. But You will be there holding my hand. You can take care of me through any storm. I love You, Lord. Amen.*

Those who worry about the future miss the joy in today! Let your loving heavenly Father handle what is yet to come. Live, love, and laugh today!

..............................................................................................................................

..............................................................................................................................

..............................................................................................................................

..............................................................................................................................

..............................................................................................................................

..............................................................................................................................

..............................................................................................................................

..............................................................................................................................

..............................................................................................................................

..............................................................................................................................

..............................................................................................................................

..............................................................................................................................

..............................................................................................................................

..............................................................................................................................

*Take therefore no thought for the morrow: for the morrow shall take thought for the things of itself. Sufficient unto the day is the evil thereof.*
MATTHEW 6:34

# Refuge in Christ

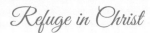

*Heavenly Father, there is no place like home. You are my home. Wherever I go in life and whatever I do, I find my refuge in You. I come before You now humbly, recognizing that You are the almighty God of the universe. And yet I can call You Abba Father, my Daddy, my Protector. Let me face this day with confidence as a daughter of the King. Amen.*

God desires a close, intimate relationship with His children. He is there to listen and to guide. Let Him be your refuge from the world.

....................................................................................................................

....................................................................................................................

....................................................................................................................

....................................................................................................................

....................................................................................................................

....................................................................................................................

....................................................................................................................

....................................................................................................................

....................................................................................................................

....................................................................................................................

....................................................................................................................

....................................................................................................................

....................................................................................................................

....................................................................................................................

*In the fear of the LORD is strong confidence:
and his children shall have a place of refuge.*
PROVERBS 14:26

# My Help Is in the Lord

*Lord, I thank You for all of the leaders and authorities in my life.
I thank You for the leaders of my country, state, and city. I pray for those
in powerful positions this morning. I pray that they might turn to You
and be led by You as they lead others. My ultimate trust is not in anyone
but You, Sovereign God. You are my hope. In Jesus' name, amen.*

Be confident that regardless of the decisions of earthly leaders,
as God's child, you will be protected by His hand.

.......................................................................................................................

.......................................................................................................................

.......................................................................................................................

.......................................................................................................................

.......................................................................................................................

.......................................................................................................................

.......................................................................................................................

.......................................................................................................................

.......................................................................................................................

.......................................................................................................................

.......................................................................................................................

.......................................................................................................................

.......................................................................................................................

.......................................................................................................................

*Put not your trust in princes, nor in
the son of man, in whom there is no help.*
PSALM 146:3

# God Hears My Prayers

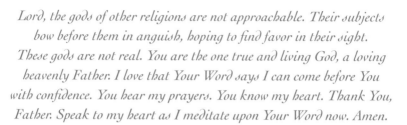

*Lord, the gods of other religions are not approachable. Their subjects bow before them in anguish, hoping to find favor in their sight. These gods are not real. You are the one true and living God, a loving heavenly Father. I love that Your Word says I can come before You with confidence. You hear my prayers. You know my heart. Thank You, Father. Speak to my heart as I meditate upon Your Word now. Amen.*

God loves you so much that He has adopted you into His family through Jesus. Go before Him with the confidence of a beloved daughter.

.......................................................................................................
.......................................................................................................
.......................................................................................................
.......................................................................................................
.......................................................................................................
.......................................................................................................
.......................................................................................................
.......................................................................................................
.......................................................................................................
.......................................................................................................
.......................................................................................................
.......................................................................................................
.......................................................................................................

*And this is the confidence that we have in him, that,*
*if we ask any thing according to his will, he heareth us.*
1 JOHN 5:14

# Avoiding Overconfidence

*God, it's easy to judge others. It's harder to take a good look at my own life. I find myself thinking, I would never. . . or How could she? What dangerous thoughts! Where I am most confident that I would never fail You, I just might. Your disciple Peter was so sure he would not betray You and yet. . .look what happened. "But for the grace of God go I" should instead be my motto. Amen.*

We are all sinners and fall short of the glory of God. Ask the Lord to protect you and keep you sharp against the devil's temptations.

........................................................................................................

........................................................................................................

........................................................................................................

........................................................................................................

........................................................................................................

........................................................................................................

........................................................................................................

........................................................................................................

........................................................................................................

........................................................................................................

........................................................................................................

........................................................................................................

*Wherefore let him that thinketh
he standeth take heed lest he fall.*
1 CORINTHIANS 10:12

## More Like Jesus

*Lord, sometimes I feel so inadequate. I fail at the very things I strive to do well in my life. I feel like the apostle Paul who said that he did the very things he tried not to do. Thank You for the promise that You aren't through with me yet! I am confident that You will continue to teach and grow me. Make me more like Jesus each passing day, I pray. Amen.*

Be confident that God is always at work in your life, making you more like Jesus—if only you will let Him.

..........................................................................................................

..........................................................................................................

..........................................................................................................

..........................................................................................................

..........................................................................................................

..........................................................................................................

..........................................................................................................

..........................................................................................................

..........................................................................................................

..........................................................................................................

..........................................................................................................

..........................................................................................................

..........................................................................................................

..........................................................................................................

*Being confident of this very thing, that he which hath begun a good work in you will perform it until the day of Jesus Christ.*
PHILIPPIANS 1:6

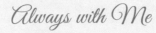

# Always with Me

*God, You have put some great people in my life. Sometimes I feel afraid that something will happen to one of them or that I will be left alone. Remind me, Lord, that You are always with me. You will be with me even if I face a great loss. You will not leave me. Help me to enjoy each day with my loved ones and not to fear the future. Amen.*

Even if you lose the dearest loves of your life, God will be there with you. You are never alone.

..................................................................................................................
..................................................................................................................
..................................................................................................................
..................................................................................................................
..................................................................................................................
..................................................................................................................
..................................................................................................................
..................................................................................................................
..................................................................................................................
..................................................................................................................
..................................................................................................................
..................................................................................................................
..................................................................................................................

*Be strong and of a good courage, fear not, nor be afraid of them:*
*for the Lord thy God, he it is that doth go with thee;*
*he will not fail thee, nor forsake thee.*
*Deuteronomy 31:6*

# More Than a Conqueror

*Father, You tell me in Your Word that I am more than a conqueror.*
*I ponder these words. What do they mean? I am more than a conqueror.*
*I am a winner. I am a chosen child of the Almighty God. I am a victor.*
*I shall see You one day. I have an abundant life and an eternal one. I am*
*more than a conqueror. I shall walk in Your strength, Father. Amen.*

God doesn't just want His people to survive. He wants us to lead abundant, joy-filled lives. He calls us more than conquerors!

........................................................................................................
........................................................................................................
........................................................................................................
........................................................................................................
........................................................................................................
........................................................................................................
........................................................................................................
........................................................................................................
........................................................................................................
........................................................................................................
........................................................................................................
........................................................................................................
........................................................................................................
........................................................................................................
........................................................................................................
........................................................................................................
........................................................................................................

*Nay, in all these things we are more than*
*conquerors through him that loved us.*
ROMANS 8:37

# Wisdom from God

*Father, the world does not have wisdom to offer me. True wisdom comes only from You. Help me today to walk as a wise daughter of the sovereign King of kings. Keep me from the temptation to listen to what the world calls wisdom. Even in times such as these, there is a remnant of Your people. We will be known by our love and by the wisdom we possess. Amen.*

The ways of the world are not the ways of the Father. Seek God. Find true wisdom.

*See then that ye walk circumspectly, not as fools, but as wise, Redeeming the time, because the days are evil.*
EPHESIANS 5:15–16

# Wise Counsel

*Help me, Lord, to know when I need to seek counsel from others. I don't want to step out, as I sometimes have in the past, on my own. I want to walk in Your ways and in Your will. Sometimes we all need help. Guide me to someone who is grounded in Your Word so that any counsel I receive will be truth. Give me wisdom, I pray. Amen.*

Younger believers should seek counsel from those who have been following Jesus longer. God has put such people in your life for a reason.

.......................................................................................................................
.......................................................................................................................
.......................................................................................................................
.......................................................................................................................
.......................................................................................................................
.......................................................................................................................
.......................................................................................................................
.......................................................................................................................
.......................................................................................................................
.......................................................................................................................
.......................................................................................................................
.......................................................................................................................
.......................................................................................................................
.......................................................................................................................
.......................................................................................................................

*The way of a fool is right in his own eyes:*
*but he that hearkeneth unto counsel is wise.*
Proverbs 12:15

# Applying Instruction

*God, give me ears to hear. Sharpen my senses and make me wise.*
*I am often proud. I think I know it all. But I don't. I need instruction*
*from You. I know this comes in many forms. . .through reading*
*and meditating on Your Word, through Your people, and through*
*circumstances. Help me to be a good listener and to apply the*
*instruction You send my way. I want to be wise, Father. Amen.*

Hearing and listening are two very different things. The truly
wise believer will apply the instruction he or she is given.
Listening well will serve you well.

........................................................................................................................

........................................................................................................................

........................................................................................................................

........................................................................................................................

........................................................................................................................

........................................................................................................................

........................................................................................................................

........................................................................................................................

........................................................................................................................

........................................................................................................................

........................................................................................................................

........................................................................................................................

........................................................................................................................

........................................................................................................................

*Hear counsel, and receive instruction,*
*that thou mayest be wise in thy latter end.*
PROVERBS 19:20

# When to Remain Silent

*Heavenly Father, Your Word says that the tongue has great power.
My words can help or harm. There are times when silence is best.
Help me to know the difference between times I should speak and times
I should keep still. I pray for wisdom as I go through this day. I want
my speech to honor You. Put a guard over my lips, I pray. Amen.*

Words can encourage or discourage. They can build trust or
they can build divisive walls. Choose your words wisely. Ask
God to guide you in this.

................................................................................................................

................................................................................................................

................................................................................................................

................................................................................................................

................................................................................................................

................................................................................................................

................................................................................................................

................................................................................................................

................................................................................................................

................................................................................................................

................................................................................................................

................................................................................................................

................................................................................................................

................................................................................................................

*In the multitude of words there wanteth not sin:
but he that refraineth his lips is wise.*
PROVERBS 10:19

# A Wise Woman

*God, others look to me as an example. I am a leader whether I want to be or not. I set the tone in my home. Give me grace and patience. Teach me how to build a home with a strong foundation rather than one that collapses when the storms come. Make my resistance strong against Satan, who tempts me to argue and isolate. Instead, find me to be a peacemaker in my home. Amen.*

God loves you. He wants your home to be a great success! Rely on Him daily to lead you as you seek to build your home on a wise foundation.

......................................................................................................................................
......................................................................................................................................
......................................................................................................................................
......................................................................................................................................
......................................................................................................................................
......................................................................................................................................
......................................................................................................................................
......................................................................................................................................
......................................................................................................................................
......................................................................................................................................
......................................................................................................................................
......................................................................................................................................
......................................................................................................................................

*Every wise woman buildeth her house:*
*but the foolish plucketh it down with her hands.*
PROVERBS 14:1

# A Calm Spirit

*Lord Jesus, I read in the Bible of the times that You expressed anger.
They were few and far between. It was a righteous anger, a godly
anger over great offenses to Your Father. I, on the other hand,
sometimes have a short fuse. I want to be wise. Fool is a strong word.
Your Word says that to have a hot temper is foolish. Replace my
anger with even-tempered responses, I pray. Amen.*

In your own strength, you will not be able to maintain a calm
spirit. With God's help, it is possible. Lean on His strength. He
wants to help you.

................................................................................................................
................................................................................................................
................................................................................................................
................................................................................................................
................................................................................................................
................................................................................................................
................................................................................................................
................................................................................................................
................................................................................................................
................................................................................................................
................................................................................................................
................................................................................................................
................................................................................................................

*A fool uttereth all his mind: but a
wise man keepeth it in till afterwards.*
PROVERBS 29:11

# Godly Wisdom

*Lord, there are so many self-help books out there now. There are even*
*therapists on TV who claim to have all the answers for our problems.*
*Not to mention the opinions of my friends and family members!*
*I read in Your Word that You were the one who put the wisdom in*
*Solomon's heart. Open my eyes that I may see. I want the wisdom*
*of God Almighty. Grant me wisdom, I pray. Amen.*

When you exhibit the wisdom of God, others will come to you
for counsel. Be ready to give an answer. Be ready to share
godly wisdom.

*And all the kings of the earth sought the presence of Solomon,*
*to hear his wisdom, that God had put in his heart.*
2 CHRONICLES 9:23

# Fear of the Lord

*Lord, there is no greater one than You. I come before You this morning as Your daughter, and yet I must not let the fact that You are my Abba Father (Daddy) negate Your holiness. You are set apart. You are good. You are all that I am not in my humanity. I am humbled, and I revere You. May my fear of the Lord be the beginning of wisdom in my spirit. Amen.*

Simply by fearing the Lord, honoring Him, declaring Him holy, you have begun on your journey toward great wisdom. Honor Him in all that you do and say today.

........................................................................................................

........................................................................................................

........................................................................................................

........................................................................................................

........................................................................................................

........................................................................................................

........................................................................................................

........................................................................................................

........................................................................................................

........................................................................................................

........................................................................................................

........................................................................................................

*And unto man he said, Behold, the fear of the Lord, that is wisdom; and to depart from evil is understanding.*
JOB 28:28

# Right Paths

*The right path is often the one less traveled. I am learning this, Father, oh so slowly. You will always lead me in the right path. You will never lead me astray. I have been at the crossroads many times, and I will face such choices again and again. Keep my heart focused on You that I might be led down pleasant paths, paths that will glorify my King. Amen.*

When you reach a fork in the road and you are not sure which path to take, stop. There is always time to pray. God will direct your heart.

..........................................................................................................

..........................................................................................................

..........................................................................................................

..........................................................................................................

..........................................................................................................

..........................................................................................................

..........................................................................................................

..........................................................................................................

..........................................................................................................

..........................................................................................................

..........................................................................................................

..........................................................................................................

..........................................................................................................

*I have taught thee in the way of wisdom;*
*I have led thee in right paths.*
PROVERBS 4:11

# God's Counsel Is Eternal

*Lord, I wish my heart was always in tune with Yours. I wish that I did not experience temptations to stray from Your perfect plan. But in truth, I struggle. There is a force within me that is fleshly and human. I feel pulled in the wrong direction at times. I know that Your counsel is eternal. It is a strong foundation on which I want to build my life. Strengthen me, I pray. Amen.*

God understands that you are human. Ever since the fall in the garden, sin has been part of the equation. Ask Him for strength. He will provide it.

........................................................................................................................................

........................................................................................................................................

........................................................................................................................................

........................................................................................................................................

........................................................................................................................................

........................................................................................................................................

........................................................................................................................................

........................................................................................................................................

........................................................................................................................................

........................................................................................................................................

........................................................................................................................................

........................................................................................................................................

*There are many devices in a man's heart;*
*nevertheless the counsel of the LORD, that shall stand.*
PROVERBS 19:21

# Grant Me Wisdom

*Lord, give me wisdom. I ask for wisdom from the one true God,
the wise One, the all-knowing, omnipotent One. You are the giver
of all knowledge. You are the way, the truth, and the life. In You,
I find the answers to life's puzzling questions. I seek You, and I
find You. As I meditate upon Your Word, instruct me, I pray.
I ask these things in Jesus' name, amen.*

God wants to give you wisdom. He blessed Solomon with great
wisdom. He will instruct you if you will seek Him. Be still
before Him. . .and listen.

........................................................................................................................

........................................................................................................................

........................................................................................................................

........................................................................................................................

........................................................................................................................

........................................................................................................................

........................................................................................................................

........................................................................................................................

........................................................................................................................

........................................................................................................................

........................................................................................................................

........................................................................................................................

*And God gave Solomon wisdom and understanding exceeding much,
and largeness of heart, even as the sand that is on the sea shore.
And Solomon's wisdom excelled the wisdom of all the children
of the east country, and all the wisdom of Egypt.*
1 Kings 4:29–30

# Amazing Grace

*Lord, I get so caught up in trying to do good works sometimes.
I need to remember that I am saved by grace. You are pleased with me
simply because I believe in Your Son, Jesus, and I have accepted Him
as my Savior. You do not bless me or withhold good gifts based on my
performance. Remind me of Your amazing grace, and make me
gracious with others. In Jesus' name I pray, amen.*

"Grace, grace. . . God's grace. . . Grace that is greater than all
our sin. . ." Rest in the calm assurance that you are saved by
grace through faith in Christ Jesus.

........................................................................................................

........................................................................................................

........................................................................................................

........................................................................................................

........................................................................................................

........................................................................................................

........................................................................................................

........................................................................................................

........................................................................................................

........................................................................................................

........................................................................................................

........................................................................................................

........................................................................................................

*For by grace are ye saved through faith; and that not of yourselves:
it is the gift of God: Not of works, lest any man should boast.*
EPHESIANS 2:8–9

# Grace with Others

*Jesus, You came to earth to live among us. You were fully God and yet fully man. You were, as the book of John says, "full of grace and truth." May I follow Your example. May I be found full of grace and truth. Give me a gracious, forgiving spirit. Grant me the discernment to see Your truth, Your light even amid the darkness of the world. Thank You, Lord. Amen.*

Just as God has been gracious with you, be gracious with others. He expects this of His children. He calls you to forgive as you have been forgiven.

........................................................................................................................

........................................................................................................................

........................................................................................................................

........................................................................................................................

........................................................................................................................

........................................................................................................................

........................................................................................................................

........................................................................................................................

........................................................................................................................

........................................................................................................................

........................................................................................................................

........................................................................................................................

*And the Word was made flesh, and dwelt among us,
(and we beheld his glory, the glory as of the only
begotten of the Father,) full of grace and truth.*
JOHN 1:14

# A Messenger of Grace

*Lord, make me a messenger of grace and peace. When I enter a room*
*and when I leave it, may grace and peace be the mark that I was there.*
*Season my conversations with these positive elements. Remove all malice*
*and gossip from my thoughts and speech. Help me to be more like Jesus.*
*I want to be a peacemaker. I want to be known as gracious. Amen.*

The apostle Paul often began and ended his letters by offering
a blessing of grace and peace. Do you bless others' lives with
grace and peace?

........................................................................................................................

........................................................................................................................

........................................................................................................................

........................................................................................................................

........................................................................................................................

........................................................................................................................

........................................................................................................................

........................................................................................................................

........................................................................................................................

........................................................................................................................

........................................................................................................................

........................................................................................................................

........................................................................................................................

........................................................................................................................

*Grace be to you and peace from God our Father,*
*and from the Lord Jesus Christ.*
2 CORINTHIANS 1:2

# Steward of Grace

*Thank You for the gifts You have given me, Lord. I look around at the other believers in my life. We are all gifted in different ways. Help me to be a good steward of the gifts You have entrusted me with in this life. Instead of looking out for myself, give me opportunities to use my abilities to minister to others. I understand that it is in doing so that I honor You. Amen.*

The world would be boring if everyone looked alike. And what if we all had the same gifts and abilities? Instead, we work together as one body with many parts.

........................................................................................................

........................................................................................................

........................................................................................................

........................................................................................................

........................................................................................................

........................................................................................................

........................................................................................................

........................................................................................................

........................................................................................................

........................................................................................................

........................................................................................................

........................................................................................................

*As every man hath received the gift, even so minister the same one to another, as good stewards of the manifold grace of God.*
1 PETER 4:10

## Unmerited Favor

*Jesus, the word grace sounds so sweet. But when I see You on that cross, bleeding, aching, dying an excruciating death, it takes on a new depth, a new meaning. You tasted death for me. You took my place. That is the grace of God. That is unmerited favor. That is unexplainable, unfathomable, and yet. . .true. Oh, Jesus, thank You for Your grace. Thank You for dying for me. I will live for You. Amen.*

Gaze at Jesus as He hangs upon the cross. That is the picture of grace. That is the epitome of mercy and love exemplified in your Savior.

........................................................................................................................
........................................................................................................................
........................................................................................................................
........................................................................................................................
........................................................................................................................
........................................................................................................................
........................................................................................................................
........................................................................................................................
........................................................................................................................
........................................................................................................................
........................................................................................................................
........................................................................................................................

*But we see Jesus, who was made a little lower than the angels for the suffering of death, crowned with glory and honour; that he by the grace of God should taste death for every man.*
HEBREWS 2:9

# Under Grace

*I am different because of grace, Father. Your free gift of salvation changes things. It sets me free. It gives me life and light and glorious joy that cannot be stolen from me. I do not have to bow to sin. It will not rule in my life. I live under the grace of Your Son, Jesus Christ. I choose to live for You and through You all of my days. Amen.*

The law was not abolished by grace, but grace made a way for us. Grace is a bridge. Step onto it. Trust it. Find your way to the Father through grace.

........................................................................................................................................

........................................................................................................................................

........................................................................................................................................

........................................................................................................................................

........................................................................................................................................

........................................................................................................................................

........................................................................................................................................

........................................................................................................................................

........................................................................................................................................

........................................................................................................................................

........................................................................................................................................

........................................................................................................................................

........................................................................................................................................

*For sin shall not have dominion over you:*
*for ye are not under the law, but under grace.*
ROMANS 6:14

# The Cross Covers Sin

*God, I recognize daily that this is a fallen world. With one bite of*
*fruit in the garden called Eden, we fell from grace. Sin entered the world.*
*We were separated from our Creator. I turn from that garden scene to*
*another scene called Calvary. What a contrast. What a gift.*
*Grace with skin on. Grace that wore a crown of thorns and bled and*
*died for mankind. Thank You, Jesus, for Your grace. Amen.*

The sin of one brought death to all mankind. The death of
Another offers life. The cross of Christ covers that bite of
forbidden fruit. . .and it covers your sin. Receive the blessing.

........................................................................................
........................................................................................
........................................................................................
........................................................................................
........................................................................................
........................................................................................
........................................................................................
........................................................................................
........................................................................................
........................................................................................
........................................................................................
........................................................................................
........................................................................................

*For if by one man's offence death reigned by one; much more*
*they which receive abundance of grace and of the gift of*
*righteousness shall reign in life by one, Jesus Christ.*
ROMANS 5:17

# Not by Works

*I cannot earn salvation, can I, Father? This life is packed with*
*working and earning. Hard work often equals success or reward.*
*But with You, there is unmerited favor. There is the gift of salvation*
*offered to me as just that, a gift. For what kind of God would You be*
*if You offered a gift and asked for payment in return? I am saved*
*by the great fullness of grace and grace alone. Amen.*

If you stacked up all your good works, wouldn't you also have
a sin stack to present to God? Not even one sin can come
before Him. It is by grace you are saved and not by works.

........................................................................................................

........................................................................................................

........................................................................................................

........................................................................................................

........................................................................................................

........................................................................................................

........................................................................................................

........................................................................................................

........................................................................................................

........................................................................................................

........................................................................................................

........................................................................................................

........................................................................................................

........................................................................................................

*And if by grace, then is it no more of works:*
*otherwise grace is no more grace. But if it be of works,*
*then is it no more grace: otherwise work is no more work.*
ROMANS 11: 6

## Extravagant Grace

*Father, You poured out Your grace. The gift of Your Son was an extravagant gift. It was of deep and painful cost to You, and yet You gave it with reckless abandon. You didn't think twice. Often I am stingy with grace. I sprinkle it. I offer it in drips or tiny tastes. I want to be generous with grace. I want it to overflow from my life. Change my heart, I pray. Amen.*

When a believer truly begins to grasp the grace of God, he or she will offer grace more freely to others. It is a natural outgrowth of salvation.

........................................................................................................
........................................................................................................
........................................................................................................
........................................................................................................
........................................................................................................
........................................................................................................
........................................................................................................
........................................................................................................
........................................................................................................
........................................................................................................
........................................................................................................
........................................................................................................
........................................................................................................

*And the grace of our Lord was exceeding abundant with faith and love which is in Christ Jesus.*
1 TIMOTHY 1:14

# An Heir to the King

*Heavenly Father, thank You for adopting me as an heir to the King of kings! You provided a way for me to come before You, Holy God. Christ carried my sin as His burden. It was nailed to the cross and has been forgiven forever, once and for all. Thank You for the abundant life that is mine because I am Yours. I praise You for viewing me through a lens called grace. Amen.*

When God looks at you, He sees you through a "Jesus lens." He sees you as righteous and pure because His Son resides in your heart.

..................................................................................................
..................................................................................................
..................................................................................................
..................................................................................................
..................................................................................................
..................................................................................................
..................................................................................................
..................................................................................................
..................................................................................................
..................................................................................................
..................................................................................................
..................................................................................................
..................................................................................................
..................................................................................................

*That being justified by his grace, we should be made heirs according to the hope of eternal life.*
Titus 3:7

# Loving My Enemies

*Lord, some of Your commands are easy to understand, such as taking care of widows and orphans. But some of them go against human nature.*
*It's easier to show mercy to those we love, but You tell us to love our enemies. You command us to love those who are hard to love. Give me a love for the unlovable, Father. I want to have a heart that pleases You. Amen.*

God loves you on your worst day just as much as He loves you when you are at your best. Extend grace to others. Practice unconditional mercy.

..........................................................................................................................
..........................................................................................................................
..........................................................................................................................
..........................................................................................................................
..........................................................................................................................
..........................................................................................................................
..........................................................................................................................
..........................................................................................................................
..........................................................................................................................
..........................................................................................................................
..........................................................................................................................
..........................................................................................................................

*For if ye love them which love you, what reward have ye? do not even the publicans the same? And if ye salute your brethren only, what do ye more than others? do not even the publicans so?*
MATTHEW 5:46–47

# Hope for the Future

*Lord, I can't see the future. I see only one piece of the puzzle at a time, but You see the finished product. As I go through this day, I will not fear because You are in control. When things seem hopeless, there is hope. My hope is in a sovereign God who says He knows the plans He has for me. I am counting on You to see me through. Amen.*

When a door closes in your life, remember that God is in control, and He knows the plans He has for you. He always has your best interest at heart.

.................................................................................................................
.................................................................................................................
.................................................................................................................
.................................................................................................................
.................................................................................................................
.................................................................................................................
.................................................................................................................
.................................................................................................................
.................................................................................................................
.................................................................................................................
.................................................................................................................
.................................................................................................................
.................................................................................................................
.................................................................................................................

*For I know the thoughts that I think toward you, saith the LORD, thoughts of peace, and not of evil, to give you an expected end.*
JEREMIAH 29:11

## Finding Hope in Scripture

*Thank You, heavenly Father, for Your holy Word. The scriptures,*
*which were inspired by You and written long ago, remain today.*
*As I read and meditate upon scripture today, I ask that You fill me*
*with hope. Comfort me through Your Word. Encourage my spirit.*
*Strengthen me for the tasks that lay ahead of me today.*
*And instruct me in the ways You would have me to go. Amen.*

The Bible is not just an old book. It is filled with God-breathed,
holy words of instruction and comfort. Find hope in God's
Word today.

.......................................................................................................
.......................................................................................................
.......................................................................................................
.......................................................................................................
.......................................................................................................
.......................................................................................................
.......................................................................................................
.......................................................................................................
.......................................................................................................
.......................................................................................................
.......................................................................................................
.......................................................................................................

*For whatsoever things were written aforetime were written*
*for our learning, that we through patience and*
*comfort of the scriptures might have hope.*
ROMANS 15:4

# Reason to Hope

*God, this world seems hopeless. People let me down. They are only human. I let them down as well. Life brings disappointments and rejections. I am thankful that You are faithful and true. You are not like men and women. What You say You will do, You always do. You are true to Your Word. You have said that I am Your child and that You will never leave me. You are my hope! Amen.*

God does not lie. It is not in His character to do so. Therefore, you can bank on every promise in the Bible. Claim some of them today!

.......................................................................................................................................

.......................................................................................................................................

.......................................................................................................................................

.......................................................................................................................................

.......................................................................................................................................

.......................................................................................................................................

.......................................................................................................................................

.......................................................................................................................................

.......................................................................................................................................

.......................................................................................................................................

.......................................................................................................................................

*God is not a man, that he should lie; neither the son of man, that he should repent: hath he said, and shall he not do it? or hath he spoken, and shall he not make it good?*
NUMBERS 23:19

# Hope in God

*Heavenly Father, when I lose my hope, You restore it. When I am depressed, You bring the smile back to my face. Even when my circumstances are not quite as I would wish, I will "yet praise" You, as did the psalmist. I will choose to hope in Christ Jesus. Quiet my soul, Father. Restore health to my countenance. I will yet praise You. I will find hope in Your promises. Amen.*

Jesus understands that life is not easy. He lived here on earth Himself! He is always there, ready to comfort you through His presence and His Word. Find hope in Christ today.

.......................................................................................................................

.......................................................................................................................

.......................................................................................................................

.......................................................................................................................

.......................................................................................................................

.......................................................................................................................

.......................................................................................................................

.......................................................................................................................

.......................................................................................................................

.......................................................................................................................

.......................................................................................................................

*Why art thou cast down, O my soul? and why art thou disquieted within me? hope in God: for I shall yet praise him, who is the health of my countenance, and my God.*
PSALM 43:5

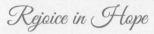

# Rejoice in Hope

*Lord, I rejoice in hope. I will be patient in tribulations. I will pray constantly. I will follow this guide from Your Word. I know that this is what You desire for me as Your child. You want me to have an abundant, joyful life in Christ. You want me to trust You as trials come into my life. And You desire an intimate relationship with me that is nurtured through prayer. Amen.*

God calls us to rejoice in hope, to be patient in times of trial, and to pray at all times. Release your burdens to Him. He is a big God.

..................................................................................................
..................................................................................................
..................................................................................................
..................................................................................................
..................................................................................................
..................................................................................................
..................................................................................................
..................................................................................................
..................................................................................................
..................................................................................................
..................................................................................................
..................................................................................................
..................................................................................................

*Rejoicing in hope; patient in tribulation;*
*continuing instant in prayer.*
ROMANS 12:12

# A Testimony of Hope

*God, hopeful people stand out in a hopeless world. When others notice my ability to face trials without giving up, may I give a reason for it. That reason is You. Without my faith, I would be lost and without any hope. With it, I am able to maintain an inner joy even in the midst of tough situations. May my life be a testimony to the hope found only in Christ Jesus! Amen.*

With gentleness and respect, be ready to testify to the power of Christ in your life. Jesus is the source of hope for the hopeless.

........................................................................................................

........................................................................................................

........................................................................................................

........................................................................................................

........................................................................................................

........................................................................................................

........................................................................................................

........................................................................................................

........................................................................................................

........................................................................................................

........................................................................................................

........................................................................................................

*But sanctify the Lord God in your hearts: and be ready always to give an answer to every man that asketh you a reason of the hope that is in you with meekness and fear.*
1 PETER 3:15

# All I Need

*Heavenly Father, You are a God of hope, joy, and great love. I don't need signs or wonders. I often wait for people or situations to turn from hopeless to hopeful. But my hope is in You. I need not wait for anything else or look for some other source. I quiet myself before You this morning and ask that You renew the hope within my heart. Thank You, Father. Amen.*

What more could anyone ask for than to be a child of the living God? We have the promise of abundant life and the hope of eternal life in heaven!

*And now, Lord, what wait I for?*
*my hope is in thee.*
PSALM 39:7

# The Hope of Heaven

*God, I cannot even imagine heaven. But I know it will be a glorious place. I know that there will be no more tears there. You tell me that in Your Word. Even the sweetest worship of my God that I take part in on this earth is nothing like the worship there. Constantly, we will worship You, Father! You have prepared a place for me there. What hope I have in You. Amen.*

Death has no power over the Christian. Because of Christ's death and resurrection, death has lost its sting! We have the hope of heaven.

........................................................................................

........................................................................................

........................................................................................

........................................................................................

........................................................................................

........................................................................................

........................................................................................

........................................................................................

........................................................................................

........................................................................................

........................................................................................

........................................................................................

........................................................................................

........................................................................................

*In my Father's house are many mansions: if it were not so, I would have told you. I go to prepare a place for you.*
JOHN 14:2

# The Return of Jesus Christ

*Jesus, I know that You will return. I find great hope in the scriptures that give a preview of that day! We don't know everything about it. We certainly cannot predict the timing of it. But the Bible assures us that You are coming back! This world is temporal. It shall all pass away one day. I am so thankful that I know beyond a shadow of a doubt that my Savior is coming back. Amen.*

The Bible says that as lightning that comes from the east is visible in the west, so shall the second coming of Christ be! He is coming again.

.................................................................................................

.................................................................................................

.................................................................................................

.................................................................................................

.................................................................................................

.................................................................................................

.................................................................................................

.................................................................................................

.................................................................................................

.................................................................................................

.................................................................................................

.................................................................................................

*And then shall they see the Son of man coming in the clouds with great power and glory. And then shall he send his angels, and shall gather together his elect from the four winds, from the uttermost part of the earth to the uttermost part of heaven.*
MARK 13:26–27

# Love in Deed and Truth

*Father, it is easy to say the words "I love you," but it is harder to live them. You want Your children to love their enemies. You tell us to love through action and with truth. These are high callings that require Your Holy Spirit working in us. Use me as a vessel of love today in my little corner of the world. Let me love through my deeds and not just with words. Amen.*

Saying "I love you" should mean something. Love is a powerful word. Be sure that your actions back up the saying when you use it.

......................................................................................................................
......................................................................................................................
......................................................................................................................
......................................................................................................................
......................................................................................................................
......................................................................................................................
......................................................................................................................
......................................................................................................................
......................................................................................................................
......................................................................................................................
......................................................................................................................
......................................................................................................................
......................................................................................................................
......................................................................................................................

*My little children, let us not love in word, neither in tongue; but in deed and in truth.*
1 JOHN 3:18

# Love Covers Sins

*Lord, all of my sin was nailed to the cross when Your Son died for me. Without grace, I am but filthy rags before a holy God. But through Christ, I am adopted as Your daughter, forgiven. There is pride in this daughter, God. Pride that resists forgiveness. Pride that says "I am right." Remind me of the multitude of my own sins that Your love covered through Jesus. Help me to love others well. Amen.*

Unforgiveness rarely hurts the other person as much as it hurts the one who refuses to forgive. Love is at the heart of forgiveness.

.........................................................................................................
.........................................................................................................
.........................................................................................................
.........................................................................................................
.........................................................................................................
.........................................................................................................
.........................................................................................................
.........................................................................................................
.........................................................................................................
.........................................................................................................
.........................................................................................................
.........................................................................................................
.........................................................................................................
.........................................................................................................

*Hatred stirreth up strifes: but love covereth all sins.*
PROVERBS 10:12

# The Love of a True Friend

*God, I am thankful for friends in my life who are more like family.*
*They accept me as I am, and yet they help me to grow. When times*
*are bad, they are there. They stick it out with me. They call.*
*They show up. They listen. They encourage. Friends like this are*
*few and far between. Thank You, Father, for friends who love*
*at all times. Make me such a friend as well. Amen.*

Do you have a friend in need? Find a way today to bless that
friend. Instead of asking what you can do, just do something. It
will mean so much.

*A friend loveth at all times,*
*and a brother is born for adversity.*
PROVERBS 17:17

# Better Than Life

*I praise You, Father, for who You are! Your lovingkindness exceeds that of any human. You are good. You are beautiful. You are all things right and true. In You and through You, all things take their shape. This world is Your creation, and You choose to keep the Earth turning on its axis. You bless us when we do not deserve blessing. Your love is better than life! Amen.*

Consider your greatest desires. Think of all the dreams you have for your future. God is greater than anything else. Keep Him central in your life.

.......................................................................................................
.......................................................................................................
.......................................................................................................
.......................................................................................................
.......................................................................................................
.......................................................................................................
.......................................................................................................
.......................................................................................................
.......................................................................................................
.......................................................................................................
.......................................................................................................
.......................................................................................................

*Because thy lovingkindness is better than life, my lips shall praise thee.*
PSALM 63:3

# Showing That I Love God

*How do I show that I love You, God? It must be more than merely a phrase I use in prayer. The way I show it is to keep Your commandments. I need Your strength for this. I fail every day. Renew my desire to live according to Your principles. They are not suggestions. They are commands. Honoring them will cause me to see You at work in my life. I love You, Lord. Amen.*

Do you know God's commandments for your life? They are in His Word. We have access to them in scripture. God desires that we keep the commands He has given.

........................................................................................................

........................................................................................................

........................................................................................................

........................................................................................................

........................................................................................................

........................................................................................................

........................................................................................................

........................................................................................................

........................................................................................................

........................................................................................................

........................................................................................................

*He that hath my commandments, and keepeth them, he it is that loveth me: and he that loveth me shall be loved of my Father, and I will love him, and will manifest myself to him.*
JOHN 14:21

# All of Me

*When You were asked what the greatest commandment was,*
*You did not evade the question. You answered clearly, Jesus.*
*I am to love the Lord my God with all of my heart, soul, mind,*
*and strength. I am to love my God with all of me. There should*
*be nothing left over when I am finished loving God. No crumbs I*
*feed to the idols that crave my attention. It is all for You. Amen.*

Where do you spend most of your time? Your money? Your
attention? Are you loving the Lord your God with all of your
heart, soul, mind, and strength?

........................................................................................................................

........................................................................................................................

........................................................................................................................

........................................................................................................................

........................................................................................................................

........................................................................................................................

........................................................................................................................

........................................................................................................................

........................................................................................................................

........................................................................................................................

........................................................................................................................

*And Jesus answered him, The first of all the commandments is, Hear,*
*O Israel; The Lord our God is one Lord: And thou shalt love the Lord thy*
*God with all thy heart, and with all thy soul, and with all thy mind,*
*and with all thy strength: this is the first commandment.*
MARK 12:29–30

# Loving My Neighbors

*Jesus, You did not stop with the first commandment. The second is strong as well. You tell me to love my neighbor. But You don't stop there. You tell me to love my neighbor as myself. But my neighbors are not always easy to love! Still, this is Your command. You have given me Your Holy Spirit. May I love with Your Spirit, for my own is lacking. Amen.*

Consider who your neighbors are. They are not just the people who live on either side of your home. Your neighbors include all the people in your life. Love them well.

.................................................................................................................................

.................................................................................................................................

.................................................................................................................................

.................................................................................................................................

.................................................................................................................................

.................................................................................................................................

.................................................................................................................................

.................................................................................................................................

.................................................................................................................................

.................................................................................................................................

.................................................................................................................................

.................................................................................................................................

.................................................................................................................................

*And the second is like, namely this, Thou shalt love thy neighbour as thyself. There is none other commandment greater than these.*

MARK 12:31

# Only One Master

*Father, there are so many things in this world that fight for my affection. It seems there is always a new product or style that the advertisements say I can't live without! It is easy to get caught up in materialism. Guard my heart, Father, and guard even my tongue. Remind me that the word love should not be used loosely. I love You, Father. Be Lord of my life, I pray. Amen.*

Do you catch yourself uttering "I love. . ." statements about the latest fashions or a yummy dessert? Consider the power of those words. Perhaps reserve them for things that really matter.

........................................................................................................................

........................................................................................................................

........................................................................................................................

........................................................................................................................

........................................................................................................................

........................................................................................................................

........................................................................................................................

........................................................................................................................

........................................................................................................................

........................................................................................................................

........................................................................................................................

........................................................................................................................

*No man can serve two masters: for either he will hate the one, and love the other; or else he will hold to the one, and despise the other. Ye cannot serve God and mammon.*
MATTHEW 6:24

# Love Is of God

*God, how will others know that I am a Christian? They will know it by my love. As I go through this day, give me opportunities to express love. It may be through a kind word of encouragement, an act of kindness, or even just a smile. Put the people in my path and on my heart today who need to experience Your love through me. Use me as a vessel of Your love. Amen.*

The words of an old song put it this way: "And they'll know we are Christians by our love, by our love. Yes, they'll know we are Christians by our love."

........................................................................................................................
........................................................................................................................
........................................................................................................................
........................................................................................................................
........................................................................................................................
........................................................................................................................
........................................................................................................................
........................................................................................................................
........................................................................................................................
........................................................................................................................
........................................................................................................................
........................................................................................................................
........................................................................................................................
........................................................................................................................

*Beloved, let us love one another: for love is of God; and every one that loveth is born of God, and knoweth God.*
1 JOHN 4:7

# A Thankful Heart

*Lord, everything good in my life comes from You. Often I forget to thank You. I am thankful for Your provision and Your protection. I am thankful for my family and friends. I am most of all thankful for the joy of my salvation, which comes through Christ. Give me a grateful heart, I pray. Let me always remember that every good and perfect gift comes from Your hand. Amen.*

A thankful heart will take you a long way in life. Try writing down three things you are thankful for at the start or close of each day.

..........................................................................................................
..........................................................................................................
..........................................................................................................
..........................................................................................................
..........................................................................................................
..........................................................................................................
..........................................................................................................
..........................................................................................................
..........................................................................................................
..........................................................................................................
..........................................................................................................
..........................................................................................................
..........................................................................................................

*And let the peace of God rule in your hearts, to the which also ye are called in one body; and be ye thankful.*
COLOSSIANS 3:15

# Blessing for Resisting Temptation

*Father, help me to resist temptation today. Every day I am tempted to sin in different ways. As I am still before You this morning, ready my heart and mind for battle. I am a warrior in this world. I know that in Your strength, I can overcome the temptations I face. Thank You for the promise that You will bless me with the crown of life. I love You, Lord. Amen.*

Don't try to resist temptation on your own. When you are tempted to sin, remember to take every thought captive to Christ.

...........................................................................................

...........................................................................................

...........................................................................................

...........................................................................................

...........................................................................................

...........................................................................................

...........................................................................................

...........................................................................................

...........................................................................................

...........................................................................................

...........................................................................................

...........................................................................................

...........................................................................................

*Blessed is the man that endureth temptation:
for when he is tried, he shall receive the crown of life,
which the Lord hath promised to them that love him.*
JAMES 1:12

# Blessing Others

*Words of blessing and encouragement from other believers mean so much to me. Help me, Lord, to be generous in my blessings to those whom You have placed within my circle of influence. Often, I pray for friends and family members privately, but I know how much it means to me when a blessing is spoken in my presence. Help me to bless others and to encourage them along their journeys. Amen.*

When someone presents you with a problem, ask if you might pray right then! The Bible tells us that where two or more gather in His name, there He is also.

...........................................................................................................................

...........................................................................................................................

...........................................................................................................................

...........................................................................................................................

...........................................................................................................................

...........................................................................................................................

...........................................................................................................................

...........................................................................................................................

...........................................................................................................................

...........................................................................................................................

...........................................................................................................................

...........................................................................................................................

*The Lord bless thee, and keep thee: The Lord make his face shine upon thee, and be gracious unto thee: The Lord lift up his countenance upon thee, and give thee peace.*
NUMBERS 6:24–26

# Blessing for Walking with God

*Give me strength, Father, to stand up for what I believe in and not just go along with the crowd. While I am in the world, as a Christian I am certainly not of it. I must guard my heart and walk in Your ways. Protect me from those who would attempt to lead me astray, I ask. Even if it means that I must endure persecution, I will walk with You, God. Amen.*

Those who are closest in your life will have great influence on you. You will be blessed if you choose to walk in the counsel of the godly rather than the ungodly.

..................................................................................................................

..................................................................................................................

..................................................................................................................

..................................................................................................................

..................................................................................................................

..................................................................................................................

..................................................................................................................

..................................................................................................................

..................................................................................................................

..................................................................................................................

..................................................................................................................

..................................................................................................................

..................................................................................................................

..................................................................................................................

*Blessed is the man that walketh not in the counsel of the ungodly, nor standeth in the way of sinners, nor sitteth in the seat of the scornful.*
PSALM 1:1

# Blessed for Keeping God's Word

*Hearing and doing are two separate things. I see this when I watch a two-year-old child at play. He hears his mother say no to something that may harm him but turns and attempts the act anyway. I do this with You sometimes, don't I, God? I read Your Word and understand it, but I go my own way. I try it alone. Help me to hear Your Word. . .and keep it. Amen.*

To truly digest scripture, you must read it and spend time meditating on it. Set aside time each day to spend in God's Word.

..................................................................................................

..................................................................................................

..................................................................................................

..................................................................................................

..................................................................................................

..................................................................................................

..................................................................................................

..................................................................................................

..................................................................................................

..................................................................................................

..................................................................................................

..................................................................................................

..................................................................................................

..................................................................................................

..................................................................................................

*But he said, Yea rather, blessed are they
that hear the word of God, and keep it.*
LUKE 11:28

# Blessed in Mourning

*Jesus, You spoke to the people on the hillside that day. How I wish I could have seen and heard You. But I have in the Bible a record of what You said. You said that I will be comforted in times of mourning. You called me blessed. Sometimes I feel that no one understands the deep loss I have experienced. Thank You for this promise. It shows me how much You care. Amen.*

In just nine statements regarding blessing in His Sermon on the Mount, Christ found it important to address those who mourn. He cares about your grief.

.................................................................................................................

.................................................................................................................

.................................................................................................................

.................................................................................................................

.................................................................................................................

.................................................................................................................

.................................................................................................................

.................................................................................................................

.................................................................................................................

.................................................................................................................

.................................................................................................................

.................................................................................................................

.................................................................................................................

.................................................................................................................

*Blessed are they that mourn: for they shall be comforted.*
Matthew 5:4

# Hungering and Thirsting for Righteousness

*Father, even as I hunger and thirst for righteousness, sometimes I am distracted. Sometimes I only halfheartedly seek You. But I do long to live as You wish for me to live. I know that through Christ, You see me as righteous. Help me to deeply desire to resist sin and to know You and glorify You fully in this life. I know that blessing comes with this type of pursuit of holiness. Amen.*

Seek Christ daily. Seek Him with your whole heart. A real, intimate, growing relationship with Him will lead you to right living and right choices.

........................................................................................................................

........................................................................................................................

........................................................................................................................

........................................................................................................................

........................................................................................................................

........................................................................................................................

........................................................................................................................

........................................................................................................................

........................................................................................................................

........................................................................................................................

........................................................................................................................

........................................................................................................................

........................................................................................................................

........................................................................................................................

*Blessed are they which do hunger and thirst
after righteousness: for they shall be filled.*
MATTHEW 5:6

## Blessed for Persecution

*Father, I have never known real persecution. I have not been thrown into prison or had my life threatened for proclaiming Christ. But there are times when others don't understand my choices. They think I am being old-fashioned. It hurts. Thank You for declaring a blessing over me when I take a stand in Your name. If I am ever truly persecuted for my faith in Christ, give me strength to withstand it. Amen.*

It is okay if people do not understand or respect the choices that you make based on God's Word. God will bless you when you take a stand.

*Blessed are ye, when men shall revile you, and persecute you, and shall say all manner of evil against you falsely, for my sake.*
MATTHEW 5:11

# Blessing Those Who Hurt You

*God, when someone hurts me, I don't feel like blessing him or her.*
*Remind me what Your Word teaches about love. Love keeps no record*
*of wrongs. Love forgives. It restores. Love tries again. Love lets it go.*
*Love blesses even when it's not my turn to bless! Give me a spirit*
*of love that trumps evil. And allow me to bless those who hurt me.*
*I can only do so in Your power. Amen.*

It is easy to lash out or to just walk away when you are hurt. It takes the power of Christ in you to bless someone who causes you pain.

........................................................................................................................
........................................................................................................................
........................................................................................................................
........................................................................................................................
........................................................................................................................
........................................................................................................................
........................................................................................................................
........................................................................................................................
........................................................................................................................
........................................................................................................................
........................................................................................................................
........................................................................................................................

*Not rendering evil for evil, or railing for railing:*
*but contrariwise blessing; knowing that ye are*
*thereunto called, that ye should inherit a blessing.*
1 PETER 3:9

# A Blessed Memory

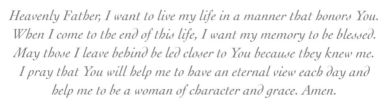

*Heavenly Father, I want to live my life in a manner that honors You.*
*When I come to the end of this life, I want my memory to be blessed.*
*May those I leave behind be led closer to You because they knew me.*
*I pray that You will help me to have an eternal view each day and*
*help me to be a woman of character and grace. Amen.*

How will you be remembered? You can impact the world for
Christ or you can live for yourself. You can encourage others or
discourage them.

..................................................................................................................

..................................................................................................................

..................................................................................................................

..................................................................................................................

..................................................................................................................

..................................................................................................................

..................................................................................................................

..................................................................................................................

..................................................................................................................

..................................................................................................................

..................................................................................................................

..................................................................................................................

..................................................................................................................

..................................................................................................................

*The memory of the just is blessed:*
*but the name of the wicked shall rot.*
PROVERBS 10:7

# Bless His Name

*Jesus, You alone are worthy of all of my praise. I bless Your name. One day I will worship You with no end, no holding back, and no earthly distraction. I will worship You in heaven forever and ever. . .with the angels and with all of Your people. For today, I go into Your world, and I will choose to bless Your name in the present. Accept my offering of praise. Amen.*

You worship Christ when you love the unlovable, when you are generous with grace, and when you share the reason for your joy and peace. Live boldly for Christ, and His name is blessed!

........................................................................................................................

........................................................................................................................

........................................................................................................................

........................................................................................................................

........................................................................................................................

........................................................................................................................

........................................................................................................................

........................................................................................................................

........................................................................................................................

........................................................................................................................

*And I beheld, and I heard the voice of many angels round about the throne and the beasts and the elders: and the number of them was ten thousand times ten thousand, and thousands of thousands; Saying with a loud voice, Worthy is the Lamb that was slain to receive power, and riches, and wisdom, and strength, and honour, and glory, and blessing.*
REVELATION 5:11–12

# Trust in God

*Heavenly Father, Your ways and Your Word are perfect and true.
I trust in You, God. You are my shield and protector. I read and
memorize Your Word so that in times of trouble, it will come to mind.
There is such power in Your Word. I will stand for what is right.
I trust in You to take care of me all the days of my life. Amen.*

Where have you placed your trust? Most things in this life will
pass away, but the Word of the Lord will stand forever. Place
your trust in the eternal God, your Creator.

......................................................................................................................

......................................................................................................................

......................................................................................................................

......................................................................................................................

......................................................................................................................

......................................................................................................................

......................................................................................................................

......................................................................................................................

......................................................................................................................

......................................................................................................................

......................................................................................................................

......................................................................................................................

......................................................................................................................

......................................................................................................................

*As for God, his way is perfect; the word of the LORD is tried:
he is a buckler to all them that trust in him.*
2 SAMUEL 22:31

*Father, I must resist the urge to put my trust in anything that is of this world. I will trust in the name of the Lord, my God. I don't need a fancy car or house. It doesn't matter if I have a lot of friends or just a few. I will place my trust in You, and You will see me through in this life. I love You, Lord. Thank You for being trustworthy. Amen.*

On April 15, 1911, the "unsinkable" *Titanic*—carrying only enough lifeboats to save approximately half of its passengers—collided with an iceberg and sank in the North Atlantic Ocean. Surely no one at the time thought that would happen! Be sure that your foundation is Christ Jesus.

.................................................................................................................
.................................................................................................................
.................................................................................................................
.................................................................................................................
.................................................................................................................
.................................................................................................................
.................................................................................................................
.................................................................................................................
.................................................................................................................
.................................................................................................................
.................................................................................................................
.................................................................................................................
.................................................................................................................
.................................................................................................................

*Some trust in chariots, and some in horses:*
*but we will remember the name of the LORD our God.*
PSALM 20:7

# God Knows

*Father, You are always watching over us. You are aware of all things.*
*You know Your children by name. I love the scripture that says You*
*know the number of hairs on my head. And because You know me*
*so well, Lord, You see that I trust in You. I will not fear trouble,*
*for You will be my stronghold when it comes. Amen.*

When you find yourself in trouble, know that God is with you.
He will give you strength to face the darkest of days if you trust
in Him.

........................................................................................................................

........................................................................................................................

........................................................................................................................

........................................................................................................................

........................................................................................................................

........................................................................................................................

........................................................................................................................

........................................................................................................................

........................................................................................................................

........................................................................................................................

........................................................................................................................

........................................................................................................................

........................................................................................................................

........................................................................................................................

*The LORD is good, a strong hold in the day of trouble;*
*and he knoweth them that trust in him.*
NAHUM 1:7

# Trustworthy through the Ages

*Lord, so many have come before me who have trusted in Your name. I read about the heroes and heroines of the Bible. They were ordinary men and women whom You used in extraordinary ways. Noah trusted You when You told him to build an ark. Abraham trusted You when You asked him to sacrifice his beloved son, Isaac. You have proven Yourself trustworthy. Teach me to trust You more. Amen.*

Ask an older Christian to tell you about a time when God delivered him or her. He has been faithful to His children through the ages. You can trust Him!

...............................................................................................

...............................................................................................

...............................................................................................

...............................................................................................

...............................................................................................

...............................................................................................

...............................................................................................

...............................................................................................

...............................................................................................

...............................................................................................

...............................................................................................

...............................................................................................

*Our fathers trusted in thee: they trusted,
and thou didst deliver them.*
PSALM 22:4

# A Testimony

*My life is a song of praise to You, my faithful Father, the giver of life!*
*When people hear my testimony of Your goodness, may they come to*
*know You. I want others to notice the difference in me and wonder why I*
*have such joy, such peace. May I point them to You, Lord, and may they*
*trust in You for salvation. You are the way, the truth, and the life. Amen.*

Does your life look and sound like a praise song to the Father?
Are you a reflection of His love to those around you?

..............................................................................................................
..............................................................................................................
..............................................................................................................
..............................................................................................................
..............................................................................................................
..............................................................................................................
..............................................................................................................
..............................................................................................................
..............................................................................................................
..............................................................................................................
..............................................................................................................
..............................................................................................................
..............................................................................................................
..............................................................................................................
..............................................................................................................

*And he hath put a new song in my mouth, even praise unto our God:*
*many shall see it, and fear, and shall trust in the LORD.*
PSALM 40:3

# Trust in His Strength

*Lord, at times I get cocky. I step out on my own and think I've got everything under control. But then something happens that shakes my world. I find myself calling on You and hoping You will come. You always show up. You always remember me. I am Your child. Help me to trust You before I am desperate. Help me to remember the Source of my strength. Amen.*

Be careful where you place your trust. It is only through Christ that we are truly strong.

..........................................................................................................

..........................................................................................................

..........................................................................................................

..........................................................................................................

..........................................................................................................

..........................................................................................................

..........................................................................................................

..........................................................................................................

..........................................................................................................

..........................................................................................................

..........................................................................................................

..........................................................................................................

..........................................................................................................

..........................................................................................................

*For I will not trust in my bow,*
*neither shall my sword save me.*
PSALM 44:6

# A Leader Who Trusts in God

*Hezekiah was not a perfect king, Father. But he was known as a leader who trusted You. That is how I want to be known. As I live out my life on this earth, please use me as an example of one who trusts in You. This is what I want to be known for in the end. It makes all the difference in the world. Amen.*

A true believer who trusts in God stands out from the crowd. Consider those whom you lead. Do they know that your trust is in the Lord?

.............................................................................................................

.............................................................................................................

.............................................................................................................

.............................................................................................................

.............................................................................................................

.............................................................................................................

.............................................................................................................

.............................................................................................................

.............................................................................................................

.............................................................................................................

.............................................................................................................

.............................................................................................................

.............................................................................................................

*He trusted in the LORD God of Israel; so that after him was none like him among all the kings of Judah, nor any that were before him. For he clave to the LORD, and departed not from following him, but kept his commandments, which the LORD commanded Moses.*
2 KINGS 18:5–6

# In Tough Times

*Lord, I will trust You on the hardest days. When trials and tribulations come my way, I tend to doubt Your presence and Your goodness. Things can seem to spin out of control. I look up and wonder where You are in it all. But You are there. You are my God, worthy of my trust. And the trials strengthen me. They bring about patience, and patience leads to experience, and experience to hope. Amen.*

Job chose to trust in the Lord regardless of external circumstances. We must decide in the light that we will trust Him in the darkness.

........................................................................................

........................................................................................

........................................................................................

........................................................................................

........................................................................................

........................................................................................

........................................................................................

........................................................................................

........................................................................................

........................................................................................

........................................................................................

........................................................................................

........................................................................................

........................................................................................

*Though he slay me, yet will I trust in him.*
JOB 13:15

# Trust in His Guidance

*Father, this morning I come before You and I praise You. You are good and loving. You have only my very best interest at heart. Take my hand and lead me. Show me the way to go. Like a child being carried in a loving parent's arms, let me relax and trust You. I know that You will never lead me astray. Thank You, God, for this assurance. Amen.*

God will walk with you all the days of your life. Trust Him to lead you. He wants to make the crooked paths straight before His children.

........................................................................

........................................................................

........................................................................

........................................................................

........................................................................

........................................................................

........................................................................

........................................................................

........................................................................

........................................................................

........................................................................

........................................................................

........................................................................

*Cause me to hear thy lovingkindness in the morning;*
*for in thee do I trust: cause me to know the way wherein*
*I should walk; for I lift up my soul unto thee.*
PSALM 143:8

# More Blessed to Give

*Jesus, You are the ultimate giver. You gave up Your life on the cross. Help me to give on a daily basis, not just on special occasions. Give me eyes to see people in need, whether they are in need of material blessings or simply my time. Make me a generous giver of all that You have entrusted to me. May my resources and talents flow freely rather than stagnating as I hoard them. Amen.*

It is better to give than to receive. Practice extravagant giving. Give more than your excess. Give of your very best. It will always come back to you.

........................................................................................

........................................................................................

........................................................................................

........................................................................................

........................................................................................

........................................................................................

........................................................................................

........................................................................................

........................................................................................

........................................................................................

........................................................................................

........................................................................................

*I have shewed you all things, how that so labouring ye ought to support the weak, and to remember the words of the Lord Jesus, how he said, It is more blessed to give than to receive.*

Acts 20:35

# Giving in Jesus' Name

*There are so many ways to proclaim Your name, Jesus. One of them is through giving. Make my heart merciful toward those in need. Remind me that while I feel I cannot change the world, I can make a difference. Your Word points out that even the smallest gesture of kindness counts. Even when You see me offer a drink of water to one person in need, You are pleased. Show me opportunities to serve. Amen.*

The story of the Good Samaritan in the Bible is powerful. As Christ-followers, we should not be passersby but participants in meeting the needs of the poor.

........................................................................................................................

........................................................................................................................

........................................................................................................................

........................................................................................................................

........................................................................................................................

........................................................................................................................

........................................................................................................................

........................................................................................................................

........................................................................................................................

........................................................................................................................

........................................................................................................................

........................................................................................................................

*And whosoever shall give to drink unto one of these little ones a cup of cold water only in the name of a disciple, verily I say unto you, he shall in no wise lose his reward.*
MATTHEW 10:42

# A Cheerful Giver

*It is a privilege to give to Your kingdom, heavenly Father. Whether I am writing out my tithe check or giving of my time and talents on a mission trip, let me give with joy. I have learned that You provide. I cannot "outgive" my God! You are too loving, too generous, too great! Regardless of my circumstances, mold my heart that I might always give with cheerfulness. Amen.*

Don't consider the cost when you give. Instead, set your eyes expectantly on what God will do with the money you invest in His kingdom!

*Every man according as he purposeth in his heart, so let him give; not grudgingly, or of necessity: for God loveth a cheerful giver.*
2 CORINTHIANS 9:7

# Tithing

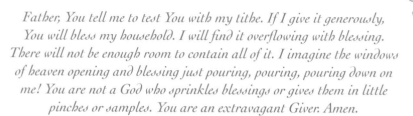

*Father, You tell me to test You with my tithe. If I give it generously,*
*You will bless my household. I will find it overflowing with blessing.*
*There will not be enough room to contain all of it. I imagine the windows*
*of heaven opening and blessing just pouring, pouring, pouring down on*
*me! You are not a God who sprinkles blessings or gives them in little*
*pinches or samples. You are an extravagant Giver. Amen.*

If you have become comfortable with giving a tenth of all your income, test God further. Give even more. There is incredible blessing to be found in giving to the Lord.

.................................................................................................................

.................................................................................................................

.................................................................................................................

.................................................................................................................

.................................................................................................................

.................................................................................................................

.................................................................................................................

.................................................................................................................

.................................................................................................................

.................................................................................................................

.................................................................................................................

.................................................................................................................

*Bring ye all the tithes into the storehouse, that there may be meat in*
*mine house, and prove me now herewith, saith the LORD of hosts,*
*if I will not open you the windows of heaven, and pour you out*
*a blessing, that there shall not be room enough to receive it.*
MALACHI 3:10

# Giving As I Am Able

*Father, Your commands are just and good. You do not demand that the poor give large sums of money that are impossible for them to attain. You ask that we give as we are able. So many times, I could give more. Show me when and how much to give. Help me to give as I am able, for that is what You expect of me, Lord. Nothing more, but certainly. . .nothing less. Amen.*

Even in times when money is short, trust the Lord and give to Him. He will bless you for remaining faithful in your tithing.

......................................................................................................

......................................................................................................

......................................................................................................

......................................................................................................

......................................................................................................

......................................................................................................

......................................................................................................

......................................................................................................

......................................................................................................

......................................................................................................

......................................................................................................

......................................................................................................

......................................................................................................

......................................................................................................

*Every man shall give as he is able, according to the blessing of the LORD thy God which he hath given thee.*
DEUTERONOMY 16:17

# Where Is My Treasure?

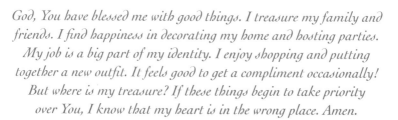

*God, You have blessed me with good things. I treasure my family and friends. I find happiness in decorating my home and hosting parties. My job is a big part of my identity. I enjoy shopping and putting together a new outfit. It feels good to get a compliment occasionally! But where is my treasure? If these things begin to take priority over You, I know that my heart is in the wrong place. Amen.*

Material blessings come from the Lord. He wants you to enjoy them. What He does not want is for them to rule you or become what you treasure most.

........................................................................................................

........................................................................................................

........................................................................................................

........................................................................................................

........................................................................................................

........................................................................................................

........................................................................................................

........................................................................................................

........................................................................................................

........................................................................................................

........................................................................................................

........................................................................................................

........................................................................................................

*For where your treasure is, there will your heart be also.*
MATTHEW 6:21

# The Ultimate Gift

*God, You gave the ultimate gift. You gave us Your only Son whom You loved so much. I can't imagine how it must have felt to watch Him go from heaven's glory to a manger bed in a lowly stable in Bethlehem. And yet, You gave Him to us freely. Out of Your great, great love for us, You sent Your Son into the world. Thank You for the gift of salvation through Jesus. Amen.*

Is there someone in your life who does not know Jesus as his or her Savior? Share Christ with that person. Tell your friend about the gift of Jesus.

..................................................................................................................

..................................................................................................................

..................................................................................................................

..................................................................................................................

..................................................................................................................

..................................................................................................................

..................................................................................................................

..................................................................................................................

..................................................................................................................

..................................................................................................................

..................................................................................................................

..................................................................................................................

*For God so loved the world, that he gave his
only begotten Son, that whosoever believeth in
him should not perish, but have everlasting life.*
JOHN 3:16

# A Legacy of Generosity

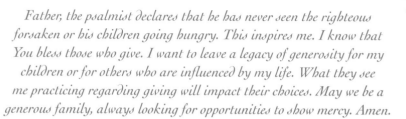

*Father, the psalmist declares that he has never seen the righteous forsaken or his children going hungry. This inspires me. I know that You bless those who give. I want to leave a legacy of generosity for my children or for others who are influenced by my life. What they see me practicing regarding giving will impact their choices. May we be a generous family, always looking for opportunities to show mercy. Amen.*

Whether you know it or not, others are watching the way that you give. Are you merciful, always looking for ways to bless those around you?

........................................................................................

........................................................................................

........................................................................................

........................................................................................

........................................................................................

........................................................................................

........................................................................................

........................................................................................

........................................................................................

........................................................................................

........................................................................................

........................................................................................

........................................................................................

*I have been young, and now am old; yet have I not
seen the righteous forsaken, nor his seed begging bread.
He is ever merciful, and lendeth; and his seed is blessed.*
PSALM 37:25–26

# A Soft Heart

*Shutting my hand is the same as hardening my heart. What a powerful warning! Father, I want to have a soft heart, one that is moved to give and to bless others. Protect me from greed that so easily could cause me to tighten my grip on my wallet. To whom You have given much, much is expected. You expect me to give freely. Help me to be a good steward of Your blessings. Amen.*

Would you rather err on the side of giving to someone whose need is not as great as he portrays or on the side of selfishness and greed?

.......................................................................................................................................

.......................................................................................................................................

.......................................................................................................................................

.......................................................................................................................................

.......................................................................................................................................

.......................................................................................................................................

.......................................................................................................................................

.......................................................................................................................................

.......................................................................................................................................

.......................................................................................................................................

.......................................................................................................................................

*If there be among you a poor man of one of thy brethren within any of thy gates in thy land which the LORD thy God giveth thee, thou shalt not harden thine heart, nor shut thine hand from thy poor brother: But thou shalt open thine hand wide unto him, and shalt surely lend him sufficient for his need, in that which he wanteth.*
DEUTERONOMY 15:7–8

# It All Belongs to God

*Lord, everything I have is Yours. The whole earth was created by You. You are the Giver of all good things, and the Bible says that You will never withhold any good gift from Your children. Lord, let me remember that it all belongs to You. I am just a manager of some of Your resources. May I use the gifts You have given me to glorify You. In Jesus' name I pray, amen.*

When you give to God, you are just giving back to Him of the great blessings He has bestowed upon your life.

........................................................................................................................

........................................................................................................................

........................................................................................................................

........................................................................................................................

........................................................................................................................

........................................................................................................................

........................................................................................................................

........................................................................................................................

........................................................................................................................

........................................................................................................................

........................................................................................................................

........................................................................................................................

........................................................................................................................

........................................................................................................................

........................................................................................................................

*And all the tithe of the land, whether of the seed of the land, or of the fruit of the tree, is the LORD's: it is holy unto the LORD.*
LEVITICUS 27:30

# The Heart of Giving

*Jesus, You see the heart of the giver. I can imagine the shock of the disciples when You declared the widow's small gift greater than that of the rich. They gave of their excess. She gave all she had. She wanted to be part of the kingdom work. She trusted You to meet her needs. May I have a true giver's heart. May I give sacrificially as the widow did that day. Amen.*

If you are not giving until it hurts, until you notice a bit of a lower bank account balance, you may not be giving enough. Give beyond the pocket change. Give sacrificially.

.......................................................................................................................

.......................................................................................................................

.......................................................................................................................

.......................................................................................................................

.......................................................................................................................

.......................................................................................................................

.......................................................................................................................

.......................................................................................................................

.......................................................................................................................

.......................................................................................................................

.......................................................................................................................

*And there came a certain poor widow, and she threw in two mites, which make a farthing. And he called unto him his disciples, and saith unto them, Verily I say unto you, That this poor widow hath cast more in, than all they which have cast into the treasury: For all they did cast in of their abundance; but she of her want did cast in all that she had, even all her living.*
MARK 12:42–44

# A Woman Who Fears the Lord

*God, I want to be a Proverbs 31 woman. My focus should not be on external beauty or the clothing and jewelry that I wear. Rather, may others notice my heart that is forever seeking You. I want nothing more than to be known as a woman of God. Protect me from vanity. Outward beauty is not lasting, but a beautiful spirit is. I meditate upon Your Word now, Lord. I want to honor You. Amen.*

Pretty clothes and makeup are not wrong in and of themselves. But remember that these things are not where your true beauty lies.

........................................................................................................

........................................................................................................

........................................................................................................

........................................................................................................

........................................................................................................

........................................................................................................

........................................................................................................

........................................................................................................

........................................................................................................

........................................................................................................

........................................................................................................

........................................................................................................

........................................................................................................

*Favour is deceitful, and beauty is vain: but a woman that feareth the LORD, she shall be praised.*
PROVERBS 31:30

## The Beauty of the Lord

*May my pursuit of You, Lord, be my "one thing." May I praise You and serve You in this life, which is but training camp for eternity! I look forward to heaven, Father, where I may truly know the depths of Your beauty. I see glimpses of Your beauty in Your creation. One day it will be fully revealed. What a glorious day that will be! Until then, be my "one thing." I love You, Lord. Amen.*

You are not a servant in your Father's house nor a traveler passing through who stays a night or two. You are a daughter of the King, and you may dwell with Him always!

........................................................................................................

........................................................................................................

........................................................................................................

........................................................................................................

........................................................................................................

........................................................................................................

........................................................................................................

........................................................................................................

........................................................................................................

........................................................................................................

........................................................................................................

........................................................................................................

........................................................................................................

*One thing have I desired of the LORD, that will I seek after; that I may dwell in the house of the LORD all the days of my life, to behold the beauty of the LORD, and to enquire in his temple.*
PSALM 27:4

# Beauty in Age

*As I grow older, Father, grant me the wisdom to see that there is beauty in age as well as in youth. You give young men strength, and certainly that is needed. They must work hard and protect their families. Some even serve in the military. But You give old men wisdom. Their gray hairs were earned through lessons learned and trials conquered. Grant me strength and mature me as I age, I pray. Amen.*

Seek wise and godly counsel when you encounter trials. Christian men and women who are older than you are a great source of wisdom.

........................................................................................................

........................................................................................................

........................................................................................................

........................................................................................................

........................................................................................................

........................................................................................................

........................................................................................................

........................................................................................................

........................................................................................................

........................................................................................................

........................................................................................................

........................................................................................................

........................................................................................................

*The glory of young men is their strength:*
*and the beauty of old men is the grey head.*
PROVERBS 20:29

# Beautiful Feet

*Oh, Lord, I imagine Your smile when You see Your people taking the Gospel of Christ into the world. Whether it is in a village on the other side of the world or right here in my neighborhood or office, may I have beautiful feet! May I carry the Gospel of Christ to others. I will run with the message, for it is life changing! How beautiful are the feet of those who bring good news. Amen.*

May we feel a sense of urgency to share the Gospel with the lost. All of heaven rejoices when just one soul is saved!

........................................................................................................

........................................................................................................

........................................................................................................

........................................................................................................

........................................................................................................

........................................................................................................

........................................................................................................

........................................................................................................

........................................................................................................

........................................................................................................

........................................................................................................

........................................................................................................

........................................................................................................

*How beautiful upon the mountains are the feet of him that bringeth good tidings, that publisheth peace; that bringeth good tidings of good, that publisheth salvation; that saith unto Zion, Thy God reigneth!*
ISAIAH 52:7

# A Meek and Quiet Spirit

*God, in Your economy a meek and quiet spirit is worth more than gold. It is not corruptible. It is eternal. Give me such a spirit. Make me into a better listener, I pray. Set a guard over my tongue at times when I should not speak. Teach me to walk humbly with You, Father, and to serve people in Your name. A gracious, godly spirit is what You desire to see in me. Amen.*

You can have a quiet spirit regardless of your personality type. God desires a kind sweetness in you as His daughter.

........................................................................................................

........................................................................................................

........................................................................................................

........................................................................................................

........................................................................................................

........................................................................................................

........................................................................................................

........................................................................................................

........................................................................................................

........................................................................................................

........................................................................................................

........................................................................................................

*Whose adorning let it not be that outward adorning of plaiting the hair, and of wearing of gold, or of putting on of apparel; But let it be the hidden man of the heart, in that which is not corruptible, even the ornament of a meek and quiet spirit, which is in the sight of God of great price.*
1 Peter 3:3–4

# Radiance

*May my countenance reflect that I am a believer, Father!*
*May people know just by the joy in my eyes that I am a*
*Christ-follower. Peace and joy are commodities of the Christian*
*that should show in their faces. I want to have such a radiance,*
*Lord. May I never be ashamed of You. May I be proud to give*
*an answer for my joy. It comes from the King of kings! Amen.*

We are to be salt and light, seasoning and illuminating. We are to shine for the Lord in this world. Is your face radiant with the joy of the Lord?

..................................................................................................................
..................................................................................................................
..................................................................................................................
..................................................................................................................
..................................................................................................................
..................................................................................................................
..................................................................................................................
..................................................................................................................
..................................................................................................................
..................................................................................................................
..................................................................................................................
..................................................................................................................
..................................................................................................................
..................................................................................................................

*They looked unto him, and were lightened:*
*and their faces were not ashamed.*
PSALM 34:5

## Beauty for Ashes

*Loving God, You alone are able to give beauty for ashes. You replace mourning with joy. Use me, in spite of the disappointments and losses I have experienced. Today is a new day. I want to be a tree of righteousness that bears good fruit, fruit that glorifies You and leads others into Your saving presence. Replace my depression with contentment and my sorrow with praise. This is my prayer today, in Jesus' name. Amen.*

In your deepest sorrow, there is still hope. In your greatest loss, God can provide a way for survival. He declares that you are more than a conqueror through Christ.

...................................................................................................................

...................................................................................................................

...................................................................................................................

...................................................................................................................

...................................................................................................................

...................................................................................................................

...................................................................................................................

...................................................................................................................

...................................................................................................................

...................................................................................................................

...................................................................................................................

...................................................................................................................

*To appoint unto them that mourn in Zion, to give unto them beauty for ashes, the oil of joy for mourning, the garment of praise for the spirit of heaviness; that they might be called trees of righteousness, the planting of the LORD, that he might be glorified.*
ISAIAH 61:3

# A Beautiful Work

*Lord, I read of the woman who poured out a flask of expensive perfume upon Your feet. The disciples did not understand, but You saw it as a beautiful work. Give me a heart like hers. Whatever I possess, whatever comes my way, help me to fling it all forth for Your glory. Let me use it wisely but extravagantly to honor my King. I love You, Lord. Make my life a beautiful work for You. Amen.*

Often what others view as too risky or outlandish is exactly what God desires. His ways are ways the world will never understand.

*But when his disciples saw it, they had indignation, saying, To what purpose is this waste? For this ointment might have been sold for much, and given to the poor. When Jesus understood it, he said unto them, Why trouble ye the woman? for she hath wrought a good work upon me.*
MATTHEW 26:8–10

# A Great Joy

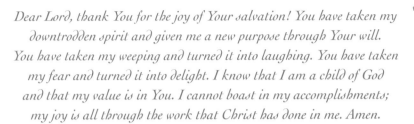

*Dear Lord, thank You for the joy of Your salvation! You have taken my downtrodden spirit and given me a new purpose through Your will. You have taken my weeping and turned it into laughing. You have taken my fear and turned it into delight. I know that I am a child of God and that my value is in You. I cannot boast in my accomplishments; my joy is all through the work that Christ has done in me. Amen.*

Today, the Lord wants you to reach down into His well of salvation and, with great joy, draw up the bucket. Remember how He saved you? Delivered you? Remember His grace? Is your bucket filled to the brim? If so, then that's something to celebrate!

........................................................................................

........................................................................................

........................................................................................

........................................................................................

........................................................................................

........................................................................................

........................................................................................

........................................................................................

........................................................................................

........................................................................................

........................................................................................

........................................................................................

*Therefore with joy shall ye draw water out of the wells of salvation.*
Isaiah 12:3

# *Eternal Joy*

*Dear Lord, thank You for the promise of heaven! I long for the day when I will be in Your presence until the end of time! What a beautiful thing that will be. Keep me focused on heaven, but remind me to stay present during my time on earth as well. Help me be a light to those around me, always pointing them toward You with my joy. Amen.*

Have you ever pondered eternity? Forever and ever and ever. . .? Our finite minds can't grasp the concept, and yet one thing we understand from scripture: We will enter eternity in a state of everlasting joy and gladness.

........................................................................................................................

........................................................................................................................

........................................................................................................................

........................................................................................................................

........................................................................................................................

........................................................................................................................

........................................................................................................................

........................................................................................................................

........................................................................................................................

........................................................................................................................

........................................................................................................................

........................................................................................................................

........................................................................................................................

........................................................................................................................

*And the ransomed of the LORD shall return, and come to Zion with songs and everlasting joy upon their heads: they shall obtain joy and gladness, and sorrow and sighing shall flee away.*
ISAIAH 35:10

# United in Belief

*Dear Lord, I place my hope in You! You are faithful, and You keep Your promises. I cannot wait to be in Your immediate presence and to be united with the entire body of believers in heaven. That will be a joyous day, and I cannot wait to raise my voice in praise with the saints! I may be bound to this earth for the time being, but I continue to long for heaven. Amen.*

When you think of standing before the Lord face-to-face, are you overwhelmed with fear or awestruck with great joy? Oh, what a glorious day it will be, when we hear Him speak those words, "Well done, thou good and faithful servant."

........................................................................................................................

........................................................................................................................

........................................................................................................................

........................................................................................................................

........................................................................................................................

........................................................................................................................

........................................................................................................................

........................................................................................................................

........................................................................................................................

........................................................................................................................

........................................................................................................................

........................................................................................................................

*His lord said unto him, Well done, thou good and faithful servant: thou hast been faithful over a few things, I will make thee ruler over many things: enter thou into the joy of thy lord.*
MATTHEW 25:21

# Complete Joy

*Dear Lord, so often I fail in keeping Your commands. I think only
of myself and my own appetites. Remind me of Your words and Your
commands. Help me to burn your law onto my heart and surrender myself
to Your will. Thank You for Your loving-kindness and blessings! Make my
heart desire You in everything, and make my joy more complete. Amen.*

Our God is bigger than anything we could ask or think. He
alone can prevent us from falling. So, if you're struggling in
the area of obedience, surrender your will. Enter into joyful
obedience.

*Now unto him that is able to keep you from falling,
and to present you faultless before the presence
of his glory with exceeding joy. . .*
JUDE 24

## Many Blessings

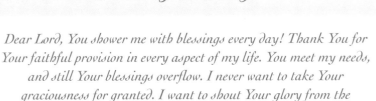

*Dear Lord, You shower me with blessings every day! Thank You for Your faithful provision in every aspect of my life. You meet my needs, and still Your blessings overflow. I never want to take Your graciousness for granted. I want to shout Your glory from the mountaintops! You have blessed me beyond measure! Thank You for multiplying my cause for joy. Amen.*

How do we praise God for His many blessings? We let others know. With a resounding voice, we echo our praises, giving thanks for all He has done, and all He continues to do. So, praise Him today! Make a joyful noise!

........................................................................................................................
........................................................................................................................
........................................................................................................................
........................................................................................................................
........................................................................................................................
........................................................................................................................
........................................................................................................................
........................................................................................................................
........................................................................................................................
........................................................................................................................
........................................................................................................................
........................................................................................................................
........................................................................................................................
........................................................................................................................

*Make a joyful noise unto the LORD, all ye lands.*
PSALM 100:1

## Forgiveness

*Dear Lord, make me willing to forgive. Help me to move past my anger and my pain, and offer a hand of friendship to those who have wronged me. This anger robs me of my joy. Show me that Your Son was willing to die for the sins of the world, offering Himself up in the ultimate act of forgiveness. I pray that I may learn from His example, and spread joy and love instead of sowing dissension. Amen.*

If you've been holding someone in unforgiveness, may today be the day when you let it go. There is incredible joy—both in forgiving and *being* forgiven.

.............................................................................................................

.............................................................................................................

.............................................................................................................

.............................................................................................................

.............................................................................................................

.............................................................................................................

.............................................................................................................

.............................................................................................................

.............................................................................................................

.............................................................................................................

.............................................................................................................

.............................................................................................................

.............................................................................................................

*Forgive us our debts, as we forgive our debtors.*
MATTHEW 6:12

## Continual Forgiveness

*Dear Lord, help me to forgive myself. I know the sacrifice that was made on my behalf by Jesus, and yet I continue to sin. The guilt keeps me from truly experiencing the joy offered to me. By accepting the forgiveness that is freely offered, I am more able to pick myself up and move on toward joy. Thank You for Your continual forgiveness and for being patient with my feet of clay. Amen.*

It's easy to get fed up with people who repeatedly hurt you and then ask for forgiveness. We grow weary with their promise that they won't do it again. If someone has repeatedly hurt you, ask the Lord to give you wisdom regarding the relationship, then ask Him to give you the capacity to forgive, even when it seems impossible.

*Then came Peter to him, and said, Lord, how oft shall my brother sin against me, and I forgive him? till seven times? Jesus saith unto him, I say not unto thee, Until seven times: but, Until seventy times seven.*
MATTHEW 18:21–22

# Infectious Praise

*Dear Lord, let my enthusiasm for praising You be infectious! I want to be a light to everyone who crosses my path. Let the joy that comes from worshiping with other believers bleed over into every aspect of my life. Whenever I worship with my fellow believers, remind me that even though we are all very different, we are all members of the body of Christ and are therefore unified in our goal and our joy. Amen.*

Are you a closet praiser? Happy to worship God in the privacy of your own home but nervous about opening up and praising Him in public? Oh, may this be the day you break through that barrier.

*And at midnight Paul and Silas prayed, and sang praises unto God: and the prisoners heard them.*
ACTS 16:25

## Guiding Prayer

*Dear Lord, thank You for always hearing my prayer. Give me the wisdom to accept Your answer, even if it is no. Father, accept my praise, feeble as it is! Being able to talk with You is a source of constant joy. Guide me on Your path, and help me to always seek Your will. I am confident that my prayers are heard. You are gracious in all things. Amen.*

In the book of Acts, it states that the early believers were constantly in prayer, in the good times and the bad. Adopt this model—take a break from the noise and spend some time with the Father.

..................................................................................................................

..................................................................................................................

..................................................................................................................

..................................................................................................................

..................................................................................................................

..................................................................................................................

..................................................................................................................

..................................................................................................................

..................................................................................................................

..................................................................................................................

..................................................................................................................

..................................................................................................................

..................................................................................................................

..................................................................................................................

*These all continued with one accord in prayer and supplication,
with the women, and Mary the mother of Jesus,
and with his brethren.*
ACTS 1:14

## Pray Confidently

*Dear Lord, I am sorry that I often treat my prayers like a grocery list. Instead of thankfulness and joy permeating my prayer, I am too caught up in the things that I want. I should know by now that You satisfy the desires of my heart. Thank You for Your patience and Your constant presence in my life. You, O Lord, are my joy. Amen.*

We don't need to come to our heavenly Father with a list in hand, but we do need to confidently approach our heavenly Father and make our requests with joy. He loves us, after all! So, draw near!

........................................................................................................

........................................................................................................

........................................................................................................

........................................................................................................

........................................................................................................

........................................................................................................

........................................................................................................

........................................................................................................

........................................................................................................

........................................................................................................

........................................................................................................

........................................................................................................

........................................................................................................

*I thank my God upon every remembrance of you, always in every prayer of mine for you all making request with joy, for your fellowship in the gospel from the first day until now.*
PHILIPPIANS 1:3–5

# Overflowing Heart

*Dear Lord, You are a just and faithful God, and that is reason for praise! Accept my humble offering and multiply my joy. You are the Creator of all things, and yet You still care about the sparrows of the field—and me. You overflow my heart with joy, and praise cannot help but bubble forth. Amen.*

Don't let anything keep you from approaching the altar with a song of praise on your lips. Today, let joy lead the way, and may your praises be glorious!

........................................................................................................................

........................................................................................................................

........................................................................................................................

........................................................................................................................

........................................................................................................................

........................................................................................................................

........................................................................................................................

........................................................................................................................

........................................................................................................................

........................................................................................................................

........................................................................................................................

........................................................................................................................

........................................................................................................................

........................................................................................................................

........................................................................................................................

*Then will I go unto the altar of God, unto God my exceeding joy: yea, upon the harp will I praise thee, O God of my God.*
PSALM 43:4

# Perfect Guidance

*Dear Lord, help me to always reach for joy. Loving others can be hard, but with Your guidance, I can love others just as You loved us first. No matter what my family looks like, I ask for Your blessing. Whether I am single or have a large family, remind me that every family has value. Help us to follow You in every way, so that the joy from salvation bleeds over into every aspect of family life. Amen.*

To obtain a joyous family environment, you've got to have a fruit-bowl mentality. Dealing with anger? Reach inside the bowl for peace. Struggling with impatience? Grab a slice of long-suffering. Having a problem with depression? Reach for joy. Keep that fruit bowl close by! It's going to come in handy!

*But the fruit of the Spirit is love, joy, peace, longsuffering, gentleness, goodness, faith.*
GALATIANS 5:22

# Blessings of Friendship

*Dear Lord, help me to be someone who encourages friendships. Instead of sowing discord wherever I go, let me instead be a beacon of joy. Put those in my path whom I can minister to, and who in turn can minister to me. I want to drink deeply from the well of friendship, so that I may know one of the greatest joys this world can afford. Thank You for this wonderful gift. Amen.*

Friendship is a privilege, and we're blessed to have brothers and sisters in Christ. But not all friendships are easy. Today, ask the Lord to show you how to "show yourself friendly" in every situation. Oh, the joy of great relationships!

..................................................................................................................
..................................................................................................................
..................................................................................................................
..................................................................................................................
..................................................................................................................
..................................................................................................................
..................................................................................................................
..................................................................................................................
..................................................................................................................
..................................................................................................................
..................................................................................................................
..................................................................................................................
..................................................................................................................

*A man that hath friends must shew himself friendly:*
*and there is a friend that sticketh closer than a brother.*
PROVERBS 18:24

# Beautiful Creation

*Dear Lord, thank You for Your beautiful creation! Nothing made by the hands of men can measure up to the majesty of the mountains, the delicacy of the lilac. Help me to be conscious of what You have done. I get so caught up in the rat race that I forget that material wealth is fleeting. Remind me of the pleasures of a simple life. My joy will be unmarred by the world. Amen.*

Imagine you're walking through a meadow on a dewy morning. The sweet smell of dawn lingers in the air. Suddenly, like a skilled orchestra, the heavens above begin to pour out an unexpected song of joy. You close your eyes, overwhelmed by the majesty of the moment. Scripture tells us the heavens and the earth are joyful. . .so tune in to their chorus today.

...........................................................................................................

...........................................................................................................

...........................................................................................................

...........................................................................................................

...........................................................................................................

...........................................................................................................

...........................................................................................................

...........................................................................................................

...........................................................................................................

...........................................................................................................

*Sing, O heavens; and be joyful, O earth; and break forth into singing, O mountains: for the LORD hath comforted his people, and will have mercy upon his afflicted.*
ISAIAH 49:13

# The Perfect Recipe

*Dear Lord, I am a selfish being. Instead of caring about the well-being of my fellow man, I get wrapped up in my own desires and I forget about those around me who are hurting. What is joy worth if it isn't shared? Help me to act with compassion and to treat others with the dignity and care that they deserve. Just as You first loved me, help me to love others. Amen.*

Want to know the perfect recipe for happiness? Spend your days focused on making others happy. If you shift your focus from yourself to others, you accomplish two things: You put others first, and you're always looking for ways to make others smile. There's something about spreading joy that satisfies the soul.

*Great is my boldness of speech toward you, great is my glorying of you: I am filled with comfort, I am exceeding joyful in all our tribulation.*
2 Corinthians 7:4

# The Right Road

*Dear Lord, help me fight off the hard grip of laziness. Show me the value in treating every task at hand as an opportunity to praise You with my work. You did not create man to be idle. Lead me down the right path, the path to joy, even if it is the more difficult path. Thank You for entrusting me with a job to do. I pray that I do it well. Amen.*

Imagine you're approaching a fork in the road. You're unsure of which way to turn. If you knew ahead of time that the road to the right would be filled with joy and the road to the left would lead to sorrow, wouldn't it make the decision easier? Today, as you face multiple decisions, ask God to lead you down the right road.

..................................................................................................

..................................................................................................

..................................................................................................

..................................................................................................

..................................................................................................

..................................................................................................

..................................................................................................

..................................................................................................

..................................................................................................

..................................................................................................

..................................................................................................

..................................................................................................

*For what hath man of all his labour, and of the vexation of his heart, wherein he hath laboured under the sun?*
ECCLESIASTES 2:22

# Deep Faith

*Dear Lord, I am anxious. I am weak, but You are strong.*
*Help me to stand strong on Your promises and to put on the*
*armor of God. You are my strength and my joy. Even when trials*
*seem too much to bear, I know that You are with me. Amen.*

Imagine a sturdy oak tree, one that's been growing for decades. Its roots run deep. It's grounded. When the storms of life strike, that tree is going to stand strong. Now think of your own roots. Do they run deep? When temptations strike, will you stand strong? Dig in to the Word. Receive it with joy. Let it be your foundation. Plant yourself and let your roots run deep.

*They on the rock are they, which, when they hear,*
*receive the word with joy; and these have no root, which*
*for a while believe, and in time of temptation fall away.*
LUKE 8:13

# Conclusion

*God's mercies are new every morning, and His holy Word is living.
It constantly brings to light wisdom and promises. Remember that there
are no "right" words that a Christian must utter in order to be heard by
God. The Lord wants to know you intimately. Go before Him in times of
joy and sorrow. Praise Him. Thank Him. Ask Him to lead you and bless
you. Pour out your heart to Him. He delights in fellowshiping with you.
You are His daughter, and He loves you with an unfailing love!*

........................................................................................................................................
........................................................................................................................................
........................................................................................................................................
........................................................................................................................................
........................................................................................................................................
........................................................................................................................................
........................................................................................................................................
........................................................................................................................................
........................................................................................................................................
........................................................................................................................................
........................................................................................................................................
........................................................................................................................................
........................................................................................................................................
........................................................................................................................................
........................................................................................................................................

*It is of the LORD's mercies that we are not consumed,
because his compassions fail not. They are new
every morning: great is thy faithfulness.*
LAMENTATIONS 3:22–23